NAPOLEON HILL

▲

ADVERSITY&
ADVANTAGE

NAPOLEON HILL

ADVERSITY&
ADVANTAGE

ACHIEVING SUCCESS
IN THE FACE OF CHALLENGES

EDITED AND ANNOTATED BY SATISH VERMA
FOREWORD BY DON GREEN

STERLING ETHOS
New York

STERLING ETHOS
New York
An Imprint of Sterling Publishing Co., Inc.

Text © 2021 The Napoleon Hill Foundation
Cover © 2021 Sterling Publishing Co., Inc.

ISBN 978-1-4549-4440-9
978-1-4549-4441-6 (e-book)

Distributed in Canada by Sterling Publishing Co., Inc.
c/o Canadian Manda Group, 664 Annette Street
Toronto, Ontario M6S 2C8, Canada
Distributed in the United Kingdom by GMC Distribution Services
Castle Place, 166 High Street, Lewes, East Sussex BN7 1XU, England
Distributed in Australia by NewSouth Books
University of New South Wales, Sydney, NSW 2052, Australia

For information about custom editions, special sales, and premium and corporate purchases,
please contact Sterling Special Sales at 800-805-5489 or specialsales@sterlingpublishing.com.

Manufactured in the United States of America

2 4 6 8 10 9 7 5 3 1

sterlingpublishing.com

Cover design by Igor Satanovsky
Interior design by Gavin Motnyk

"Every defeat, every disappointment, and every adversity
carry seeds of equivalent or greater benefits."

—*Napoleon Hill*

CONTENTS

Foreword X

Introduction xii

Before You Begin xv

CHAPTER 1: DEFINITENESS OF PURPOSE
(THE FIRST STEP FROM POVERTY TO RICHES) 1

OVERVIEW 2

BROADCAST 1. DEFINITENESS OF PURPOSE 2

WISDOM TO LIVE BY 13

ADVERSITY AND ADVANTAGE 13

CHAPTER 2: GOING THE EXTRA MILE
(A SECRET THAT CAN EXPLODE YOUR SUCCESS) 15

OVERVIEW 16

BORADCAST 2. GOING THE EXTRA MILE 16

WISDOM TO LIVE BY 31

ADVERSITY AND ADVANTAGE 32

CHAPTER 3: MASTER MIND
(THE SUPREME SECRET TO ALL GREAT SUCCESSES) 33

OVERVIEW 34

BROADCAST 3. MASTER MIND PRINCIPLE 34

WISDOM TO LIVE BY 47

ADVERSITY AND ADVANTAGE 47

CHAPTER 4: THE THREE MAJOR CAUSES OF FAILURE
(OUR GREATEST BLESSING MAY BE OUR GREATEST SORROW) 48

OVERVIEW 49

BROADCAST 4. THE THREE MAJOR CAUSES OF FAILURE 49

WISDOM TO LIVE BY 64

ADVERSITY AND ADVANTAGE 65

CHAPTER 5: HOW TO CONDITION YOUR MIND FOR SUCCESS (A WAY TO INFLUENCE YOUR LUCK, FATE, CHANCE, AND DESTINY)..........66

OVERVIEW 67

BROADCAST 5. HOW TO CONDITION YOUR MIND FOR SUCCESS 67

WISDOM TO LIVE BY..........81

ADVERSITY AND ADVANTAGE 82

CHAPTER 6: HOW TO DEVELOP POWER OF APPLIED FAITH (THE POWER BEYOND SCIENCE)..........83

OVERVIEW 84

BROADCAST 6. HOW TO DEVELOP THE POWER OF APPLIED FAITH 84

WISDOM TO LIVE BY..........100

ADVERSITY AND ADVANTAGE 101

CHAPTER 7: HOW TO DEVELOP A WINNING PERSONALITY (PREREQUISITE TO BECOME A GREAT LEADER) 102

OVERVIEW 103

BROADCAST 7. HOW TO DEVELOP A WINNING PERSONALITY..........103

WISDOM TO LIVE BY..........116

ADVERSITY AND ADVANTAGE 117

INTRODUCTION TO CHAPTER 8: SELF-DISCIPLINE (A MENTAL POWER CLOSE TO DIVINITY)..........118

OVERVIEW 119

BROADCAST 8. SELF-DISCIPLINE..........119

WISDOM TO LIVE BY..........132

ADVERSITY AND ADVANTAGE 133

CHAPTER 9: POSITIVE MENTAL ATTITUDE (A BLESSING OF THE HIGHEST ORDER)..........134

OVERVIEW 135

BROADCAST 9. A POSITIVE MENTAL ATTITUDE............................135

WISDOM TO LIVE BY......................................147

ADVERSITY AND ADVANTAGE 148

CHAPTER 10: THE TWELVE GREAT RICHES
(PATHWAY TO PEACE OF MIND)....................................149

OVERVIEW 150

BROADCAST 10. THE TWELVE GREAT RICHES............................150

WISDOM TO LIVE BY......................................165

ADVERSITY AND ADVANTAGE 165

CHAPTER 11: THE BIG FOUR (A TICKET TO FAVORABLE BREAKS).............167

OVERVIEW 168

BROADCAST 11. THE BIG FOUR......................................168

WISDOM TO LIVE BY......................................180

ADVERSITY AND ADVANTAGE 181

CHAPTER 12: FACTORS OF A POSITIVE MENTAL ATTITUDE (A PRICELESS ASSET) ..182

OVERVIEW 183

BROADCAST 12. FACTORS OF A POSITIVE MENTAL ATTITUDE................183

WISDOM TO LIVE BY......................................193

ADVERSITY AND ADVANTAGE 193

CHAPTER 13: THE GOLDEN RULE (BRINGING YOU PEACE OF MIND)...........195

OVERVIEW 196

BROADCAST 13. REVIEW 196

WISDOM TO LIVE BY......................................210

ADVERSITY AND ADVANTAGE 210

NAPOLEON HILL'S CODE OF ETHICS 211

Appendix...213

NAPOLEON HILL IS ON THE AIR

Napoleon Hill, author of many popular motivational books, including the groundbreaking *Law of Success* in 1928 and *Think and Grow Rich* in 1937, adviser to Presidents Woodrow Wilson and Franklin D. Roosevelt, and lecturer and instructor to tens of thousands of people, had begun to settle into retirement with his wife at their Los Angeles home in the 1950s. He was approaching his seventieth year and was enjoying slowing down, although somewhat grudgingly, after living such an active and prolific life. I say "somewhat grudgingly" because, though he deeply loved his wife Annie Lou, he was a restless man who believed so strongly in the success principles he had studied for nearly half a century that he wanted to see them continue to spread throughout the world.

Mr. Hill did have a few remaining speaking commitments, one being at a dental convention in Chicago in 1952. At that event he was introduced to W. Clement Stone, a longtime follower who was also giving a speech to the conventioneers. Mr. Stone, a multimillionaire insurance tycoon, persuaded him to come out of retirement and to resume his speaking and writing career full time. In 1955, Mr. Hill, in partnership with Mr. Stone, presented a series of thirteen lectures on the radio on successive Sundays in Chicago, Illinois. Fortunately, these broadcasts were recorded. They have never been published before. The recordings were only recently found in the archives of the Napoleon Hill Foundation, tucked away in a dusty box on a high shelf in a storeroom, and long forgotten.

In these programs, Mr. Hill was interviewed by Henry Alderfer, the associate director of the Napoleon Hill Institute, an organization Mr. Stone and Mr. Hill had established to teach the principles of success developed by Mr. Hill over the decades. The first three shows dealt with three of the four most important principles previously disclosed by Mr. Hill, namely, having a definite major purpose, going the extra mile, and having a master mind alliance. The sixth show dealt with the fourth such principle, applied faith. Broadcasts eight and nine dealt with two more of the seventeen success principles, self-discipline and a positive mental attitude. The remaining broadcasts diverged from focus on a single principle, dealing with such subjects as the twelve great riches of life, the factors making up a positive mental attitude in one's personality, conditioning one's mind for success, developing a winning personality, and the major causes of failure.

A theme running through many of these broadcasts, perhaps counterintuitive when first encountered, is that no one truly succeeds without first experiencing failure. One learns from failure and can put the lessons learned to good use in moving forward to achieve success. As Mr. Hill wrote, "Every adversity, every defeat, and every heartbreak carry with it the seed of an equivalent advantage." This is a powerful message, worthy of much contemplation, and these broadcasts provide many illustrations of the truth of this principle.

Delivered in the mid-1950s, while the United States (and much of the rest of the world) was still recovering from the horrors and privations of World War II and the Korean War, these messages, particularly those dealing with recovering from adversity, were especially timely. And, though presented many decades ago, they are as timely now as they were then.

The Trustees of the Napoleon Hill Foundation are proud to be preserving the memory, legacy, and teachings of Dr. Napoleon Hill and believe you will benefit from and enjoy these valuable radio programs.

As a special bonus feature, we have included as an appendix the never before published talk presented by Napoleon Hill at the Chicago dental convention in 1952, the occasion of his introduction to W. Clement Stone.

Don Green
Executive Director and Trustee
Napoleon Hill Foundation

INTRODUCTION

Napoleon Hill's work has touched and transformed the lives of millions. His success philosophy has empowered people worldwide to pull themselves out of poverty and a state of perpetual unhappiness to lead a life of abundance, achievement, and joy.

As one of the most revered and influential figures in the field, Napoleon Hill created a body of work that is as relevant today as it has been over the past eighty years. His work reveals the secrets of the minds of those who have shaped their own destiny, and the destiny of the world. Modern-day personal development gurus continue to turn to Napoleon Hill's principles for guidance and inspiration.

The great author Ben Jonson said that "Shakespeare was not of an age, but of all time." So too is Napoleon Hill's legacy in the field of personal development literature. Like Shakespeare, the depth and elegance of Hill's work is unparalleled to this day, ensuring that it will continue to inspire millions for centuries to come.

Shakespeare made language come alive with phrases such as "All's well that ends well," that are still commonly quoted today. He humanized his characters by making them so lifelike that we could easily relate to their weaknesses and strengths, their limitations and limitlessness, their failures and successes.

Similarly, Hill's phrases such as "Whatever the mind can conceive and believe, the mind can achieve," have become common currency of today's success literature. Hill's success principles were humanized through the experience of real people who, through their own stories, characterized their successes or their failures by their adherence, or lack of it, to Hill's principles.

This book is a collection of talks that Napoleon Hill delivered over the radio, explaining the basic steps by which one may overcome adversity of any kind and turn it into an advantage of greater magnitude than the adversity itself. Like his other works, it reveals the true path to enduring success for anyone who wishes to follow it.

My gratitude to Don Green, the executive director of the Napoleon Hill Foundation, who gave me the honor of annotating this masterwork. My passion for Hill's philosophy of success was born of my own experience with great personal adversity some thirty years ago.

Faced with financial ruin, as well as emotional, spiritual, and even physical challenges, I was given the life-changing introduction to Napoleon Hill's lessons and principles of success. Within six months, I had overcome bankruptcy and went on to amass wealth and live the life of my dreams.

The following discoveries I have made through the study of his work have guided me through adversity and put me on the path of enduring success:

- There are hidden forces inside all of us that, once unleashed, can give us unlimited belief in our abilities.

- Everything has a just price, which must be paid if you want to acquire anything.

- It is a great law of nature that if you make your mind focus on the image of your desire, your mind's natural habit is to do whatever it can to make your desire into a reality.

- Human thoughts have a tendency to transform themselves into their physical equivalent.

- You can tap into the power of the universe and use it to your advantage without violating the rights of others.

- A simple nightly routine can extinguish six basic fears from your life.

- There is a simple five-point formula that guarantees unbreakable self-confidence.

- You can get ideas off the ground even when you don't have any money.

- There is a secret to attracting the right people into your life.

I am confident that by following the principles in the material Napoleon Hill has laid out, this book will be as transformative for you as it was for me.

Satish Verma
President and CEO
Think and Grow Rich Institute

BEFORE YOU BEGIN

The following pages will unlock the mystery of how to overcome adversity and use it to your advantage to achieve enduring success. This mystery is revealed to you by the greatest self-improvement teacher of all time, Napoleon Hill himself.

In each chapter, Napoleon Hill talks directly to you (the chapter text is a transcript of his lessons delivered over the radio) to show you the path to conquer adversity, failure, and heartache; in doing so, you will build yourself up mentally, physically, and spiritually, so that you can achieve harmony and peace of mind.

Each chapter of Hill's original radio transcript is prefaced with additional material to guide you through the key themes and concepts pertaining to the essence of the chapter's teachings. Around the world, people have suffered hardship because they have lacked the powerful knowledge about the nature of success. Hill presents the lessons in a simple and concise way, making them easy to follow. The principles and concepts, if understood and applied consistently, will help you overcome any adversity you may encounter over your life's journey.

Each chapter concludes with annotations to the preceding lesson, featuring key takeaways about the nature of success and adversity. Reflecting on these timeless principles and applying them to your life will help you to overcome the greatest enemies of mankind, such as poverty, fear, and self-imposed limitations.

May this book bring you peace and harmony.

Satish Verma
President and CEO
Think and Grow Rich Institute

CHAPTER 1

DEFINITENESS OF PURPOSE

(THE FIRST STEP FROM POVERTY TO RICHES)

△

*"As a rule, adversity reveals genius
and prosperity hides it."*

Horace

OVERVIEW

Each of the chapters in this book provides an essential lesson on the path toward self-empowerment and a lifetime of success. Together, the chapters set out a road map that, if followed vigorously and consistently, will lead you to the life of your dreams.

The purpose of this opening chapter is to lay out the fundamental knowledge and understanding needed to take that very first step toward your destiny. Hill addresses this step as the very reason for your existence, the reason you were born, and the context of your life. Exploring this concept will free you from the limitations of fear, doubt, and discouragement.

You will learn that:

- There are no outside forces that control your destiny.

- There is one starting point of all achievement for all people.

- There is only one thing that brings you poverty and misery.

- Acquiring a single habit can help you overcome any adversity.

Millions of people have gone on to amass great fortunes armed with the knowledge presented in this chapter, and it can do the same for you. Your new life's journey begins now.

BROADCAST 1. DEFINITENESS OF PURPOSE

ANNOUNCER:
Good afternoon, ladies and gentlemen. The Radio School of Success Unlimited is on the air. The Philosophy of Success as developed by Napoleon Hill will be introduced to you in thirteen consecutive programs. This presentation of the Science of Success philosophy will be given by Napoleon Hill. The time doesn't allow me to give a complete story of Napoleon Hill's background, but his success books, *Think and*

Grow Rich and *How to Raise Your Own Salary*, are bestsellers in every nation of the world. This School of the Air presents the principles of success as developed by Mr. Hill. Assisting Mr. Hill in the School of the Air is associate director of education, Henry Alderfer. And now, here is Mr. Alderfer.

ALDERFER:
Thank you. It is indeed a pleasure to be associated with Napoleon Hill, but I am sure you would like to hear from Napoleon Hill himself. Ladies and gentlemen, Napoleon Hill.

NAPOLEON HILL:
Thank you, Henry Alderfer. Before presenting our first program, the radio audience should know our definition of the word "success." It is the ability to get everything one desires from life without violating the rights of others. By this definition, please understand that you are the only person who can determine whether or not you are a success.

ALDERFER:
Mr. Hill, is it true, as some people believe, that there are conditions beyond our control which limit us as to the degree of success we can attain? Is it true, for example, that people who are born under certain signs of the stars are eternally doomed to misery and failure?

NAPOLEON HILL:
The best answer to this question is to call attention to the fact that men and women throughout the world, people who are born under every sign of the stars, are establishing their own goals in life, and they are attaining them by the application of a success philosophy. These men and women have discovered that their limitations are those which they set up or accept in their own minds. It is very possible that anyone may become successful by following instructions and applying the Philosophy of Success.

ALDERFER:

Would it not be a very fundamental requirement for a philosophy of success to have a Definiteness of Purpose?

NAPOLEON HILL:

Definiteness of Purpose, or a specific objective in life, is the starting point of all individual success. Unless one knows what one's goal in life is, there will be no initiative to reach it. At the very beginning of the analysis of Definiteness of Purpose, let us call attention to its profound nature and its limitless power as a means of positive thinking. First of all, consider the fact that the Creator gave each of us complete power of control over but one thing, and that is the privilege of directing the mind to whatever purpose we choose. It is evident that the Creator intended us to take full and complete possession of our minds, and to direct them with Definiteness of Purpose, because we know that the person who neglects to do this is penalized through poverty, misery, and failure.

ALDERFER:

Mr. Hill, is there an appropriate reward for those who do take possession of their minds and direct their mind power to definite ends of their own choice?

NAPOLEON HILL:

Yes, there is, and you can prove this to your own satisfaction by analyzing men and women in all walks of life who have attained success by establishing definite goals. In every instance, you will observe that these successful people discovered the power of positive thinking by adopting a Definiteness of Purpose toward objectives of their own choice.

ALDERFER:

I believe our listeners will be interested in some case histories of people who have achieved outstanding success through the application of a success philosophy based upon having Definiteness of Purpose.

NAPOLEON HILL:

Very well. That's a good idea. The first one of these cases is about a man who is a personal friend, and he is very well known and highly admired by thousands of radio listeners. He is Earl Nightingale, and here is his story in his own words.

"I don't think a day has gone by in the last five years that the influence of the Philosophy of Success has not shaped my life in every way. Coming upon it as I did after years of earnest seeking for the answers was like being rescued from the sea. I experienced an illumination so brilliant as to remove all shadows of doubt. Since then, just a few short years ago, I have been able to get everything I set my mind upon. Within a week of having discovered the formula for success, I had doubled my salary, and then, just to make sure, I redoubled it. I have formed four companies since that time, and I am well on the road toward my goal in life. Incredible as it may seem, there is one bit of wisdom that has passed down from antiquity unchanged and unchallenged. Great thinkers from time's very beginning have uttered it as if it were their own personal discovery, and so it was. We can read it a thousand times and have it shouted in our faces, but for some strange self-limiting reason, we can't discover it until we are ready to discover it. 'Human thoughts have a tendency to transform themselves into their physical equivalents.' That's all. Not very exciting to look at, is it? Just twelve words that still give me the chills when I think of the power they contain."

ALDERFER:

Earl Nightingale's story is a discovery of the power within his own mind, and it corresponds perfectly with what has been said about the soundness of the idea of Definiteness of Purpose. Will you give us another case history?

NAPOLEON HILL:

Yes, and here is a very interesting case, which shows what may happen when one neglects to move with Definiteness of Purpose.

Some years ago R. U. Darby from Baltimore, Maryland, had the good fortune to discover a very rich vein of gold while vacationing in the West. He went back home and borrowed money from friends and relatives with which to install mining machinery and came back West and went to work mining the rich gold ore. All went well for a few weeks. Then suddenly the vein stopped. In sheer desperation Darby sold the mining equipment to a junk dealer for a fraction of what it had cost, and he returned home. But the junk dealer proved himself smart by calling in a mining engineer, who examined the mine, then announced that a fault in the earth had cut off the vein of ore. He said, "Dig ahead a few feet, and you will pick up the vein again." The new owner, the man with Definiteness of Purpose, dug ahead just three feet and there picked up the vein again. His Definiteness of Purpose yielded him several millions of dollars. The mine turned out to be one of the richest in the West. Every day, there are men and women, like Darby, stopping just short of a glorious success because they are drifting through life without aim or purpose.

ALDERFER:
Mr. Hill, will you give us a case history of someone else, well known to the present generation, who has attained great success through Definiteness of Purpose?

NAPOLEON HILL:
Yes. Some years ago a young college student by the name of Jennings Randolph established his major goal in life and set out to attain it immediately after becoming aware of the importance of Definiteness of Purpose. His first aim was to become a member of Congress after he had finished school. He attained that aim and served in Congress for fourteen years. Not satisfied to stop there, he established another goal that lifted him into his present position as assistant to the president of Capital Airlines, and it is quite possible that Randolph will go still higher to whatever objectives he may set his mind upon because he understands and makes full use of the principle of Definiteness of Purpose.

ALDERFER:

There are a number of important facts or premises that need to be understood in order to set up one's definite objective in life. Will you describe them for our listeners?

NAPOLEON HILL:

Two central factors are the very foundation stones upon which are built the idea of Definiteness of Purpose, and they clearly show why no one may attain success without them. Number one, the starting point of all individual achievement, is the adoption of a definite purpose, accompanied by a definite plan for its attainment, and followed by appropriate action behind that plan.

All individual achievements are the results of a motive or a combination of motives, and the basic motives that inspire all voluntary human action are as follows: the emotion of love, the emotion of sex, the desire for material riches, the desire for self-preservation, the desire for freedom of body and mind, the desire for personal expression and recognition by others, the desire for perpetuation of life after death, and then these two negatives, which are said to inspire more human action than all the other seven motives combined, namely, the desire for revenge for real or imaginary grievances and the grandfather of them all, fear.

Number two, any dominating plan or purpose held in the mind through repetition of thought and emotionalized with faith or a burning desire for its realization is taken over by the subconscious section of the mind and acted upon through whatever natural and logical means that may be available and carried out to its logical conclusion.

ALDERFER:

Will you tell our listeners what some of the major benefits are that may be obtained through Definiteness of Purpose?

NAPOLEON HILL:

Definiteness of Purpose automatically develops self-reliance, personal initiative, imagination, enthusiasm, self-discipline, and concentration of effort, all of these being prerequisites for the attainment of success. It induces one to budget one's time and to create day-by-day plans, which lead to the attainment of one's overall or major purpose in life. It makes one more alert in recognizing opportunities related to the object of one's definite major purpose. It inspires confidence in one's integrity and character, and it attracts the favorable attention of people who may aid one in the attainment of one's aims and purposes in life. It opens the way for the full exercise of that state of mind known as faith by making the mind positive and removing it from the limitations of fear and doubt and anxiety. It makes one success-conscious, this being the first step in the direction of successful achievement in all undertakings. Definiteness of Purpose also aids one in developing and maintaining a positive mental attitude.

ALDERFER:

Mr. Hill, much interest has been expressed lately dealing with the subject of a positive mental attitude, and I believe our radio audience would like to know how to develop the habit of positive thinking.

NAPOLEON HILL:

There is a formula that has been used effectively. It is a simple one, which anyone may appropriate and use without great effort. Number one, draw a clear picture in your mind of precisely what you desire, and begin to live and act as you would if your desires had already been realized. Back your desires by as many of the basic motives as possible. Keep your desires active at all times through both physical and mental actions. Inactivity in regard to desires is reckless.

Number two, set yourself into believing you will attain the object of your desires. Keep your mind off of circumstances and things you do not desire, because the mind attracts that which it feeds upon. Concentrate on the reasons why you believe you are entitled to realize the object of your desires, including that which you intend to give in return, and start giving where you stand. Form the habit of acquiring information essential for the attainment of your desires by asking questions of people whom you know to have the right answers. Keep the object of your desires to yourself lest you set up jealousies and oppositions that may beset you. Place as many people as possible under obligation to you by the habit of Going the Extra Mile, rendering more service than that which is expected of you. Keep your mind free of envy and anger and greed and hatred and jealousy and revenge and fear, because these are the seven dark sources of failure. In these instructions you have the means of developing a positive mental attitude that will attract to you the things and the people related to your aims and purposes in life.

ALDERFER:
Mr. Hill, if a person has developed a positive mental attitude, how does he work toward attainment of his definite major purpose?

NAPOLEON HILL:
Number one, write out a clear statement of your major purpose in life, sign it, commit it to memory, and repeat it at least twice daily in the form of a prayer or affirmation. If you are married, have your mate sign the statement with you and repeat it together just before retiring each night. Two, write out a clear, definite outline of the plan or plans by which you intend to achieve the object of your definite major purpose and state the maximum amount of time within which you intend to achieve it. Then describe in detail precisely what you intend to give in return for the realization of the object of your purpose. Keep in mind the fact that everything has a just price, which must be paid. Third, keep your definite major purpose strictly to yourself and your mate in marriage, except for those instances that will be brought out in a future broadcast regarding the Master Mind. Call your definite major purpose into your conscious mind as often as may be practical. Eat with it. Sleep with it. And take

it with you every hour of the day, keeping in mind the fact that your subconscious mind can be influenced to work for its attainment while you sleep.

ALDERFER:
Mr. Hill, I believe our listeners would be interested in how these thoughts that we have discussed today were acquired and developed in the Philosophy of Success and would like perhaps to understand something of the philosophy's relationship to our American way of life and our system of free enterprise.

NAPOLEON HILL:
It was begun under the sponsorship of Andrew Carnegie, the founder of the United States Steel Corporation, who commissioned me in 1908 to give the world its first practical philosophy of individual achievement. Stated as briefly as possible, it is the organized know-how of the men who have done most to develop and stabilize our great American way of life and our system of free enterprise. Mr. Carnegie gave away most of his money before his death, but he entrusted to me what he said was the greater portion of his riches, which consisted of the means by which he acquired his wealth, and he committed me to devote my life to taking this knowledge to the people of the world.

ALDERFER:
Because the story of how Andrew Carnegie came to sponsor you is so related to Definiteness of Purpose, will you describe it for our listeners?

NAPOLEON HILL:
I had my first interview with the great industrialist as a young newspaper man. I went to see Mr. Carnegie to write a success story about him. He agreed to give me three hours, but actually kept me at his home for three days and three nights, during which he was interviewing me while I was interviewing him. Without my being aware

of this fact, Mr. Carnegie was testing me to see if I had a certain quality that he knew would be needed by the man who would organize the Science of Success philosophy.

ALDERFER:

How interesting. And what was this particular quality that concerned Mr. Carnegie so greatly?

NAPOLEON HILL:

It was the one quality without which no person may achieve noteworthy success in any calling, and I may add it was a quality I did not know I possessed until it was disclosed by the searching mind of the great Andrew Carnegie.

ALDERFER:

Is this quality for which Mr. Carnegie was searching one that can be acquired, or is it one with which a person must be endowed at birth?

NAPOLEON HILL:

It can be acquired by all who master and apply the idea of Definiteness of Purpose. This quality consists of the habit of turning on more willpower instead of quitting and accepting defeat when one is faced with difficult problems and the going becomes hard. As a means of testing me on this important quality, Mr. Carnegie burdened my assignment with the condition that I earn my own way while carrying on twenty years of research without any subsidy from him. At the time I thought this condition was very cruel, but later I discovered that it was a great blessing because it forced me to become resourceful and to apply the success principles I was uncovering in my research.

ALDERFER:

What percentage of the people of the world follow the habit of applying Definiteness of Purpose, that is, how many decide on a definite goal in life?

NAPOLEON HILL:

Approximately 5 percent. The vast majority, approximately 95 percent of the people of all countries, go around and around without aim or purpose. They drift with the circumstances of life, good or bad, whereas the successful individuals create their own circumstances and ride them to victory.

ALDERFER:

Who was another famous person that was instrumental in developing this philosophy?

NAPOLEON HILL:

Thomas A. Edison was without a doubt the most interesting and the one from whom I probably received the most important aid during my twenty years of research. I mention Mr. Edison not only because of his great achievements, but because he accomplished them despite his lack of extensive formal education. Mr. Edison had that quality which got me my opportunity with Andrew Carnegie, namely, the habit of turning on more effort instead of quitting when the going was hard. Before he perfected the modern incandescent electric light, he tried more than ten thousand different ideas, all of which failed to work. Now there was a Definiteness of Purpose without a parallel in the history of mankind. It seems to me that the whole power of the universe becomes mysteriously available to the person who keeps on when he is tested by difficult problems and the going seems beyond human endurance.

ALDERFER:

It is quite evident from this illustration that the statement "whatever the mind can conceive and believe, the mind can achieve" is one of the strongest incentives to become successful by having a definite goal in view.

Thank you, Mr. Hill, for your very interesting illustrations of applications of Definiteness of Purpose. Next week we will discuss Going the Extra Mile, a principle revealing the method by which you can lift yourselves to great heights by doing more than is required and expected. Please tune in again at the same time next Sunday.

WISDOM TO LIVE BY

1. Adversity does not come to you because you failed at something. Not having a Definite Major Purpose in itself is the biggest failure of life. The most significant consequences for not having a purpose are poverty, misery, and failure.

2. Many people give up on their Definite Major Purpose because they think that their plan is not sound enough to achieve their purpose. They wait until they have a strong plan. Hill is of the opinion that any plan, strong or weak, is better than no plan. A weak plan has a way of becoming strong if definitely applied. "The difference between a sound plan and an unsound plan is that a sound plan, if definitely applied, may be carried out more quickly than an unsound plan." If one plan fails, substitute with another plan.

3. A plan must be based on just and moral motives. A plan and purpose that are not just may bring temporary success, but it will not last. Enduring success comes only when your cause is just and moral; if it is not, the consequences that follow are very heavy.

ADVERSITY AND ADVANTAGE

1. Willpower is the one quality without which no person may achieve outstanding success in any calling. As Hill teaches us, "When you face an adverse situation or failure in the process of achieving your definite purpose, just turn on more willpower instead of quitting."

2. Hill closes the lesson with a powerful statement when he says, "It seems to me that the whole power of the universe becomes mysteriously available to the person who keeps on when he is tested by difficult problems and the going seems beyond human endurance."

3. Just this one outstanding quality (willpower) will help you to discover your other-self, and that self knows no failure, no defeat, and no limitations.

▼

CHAPTER 2

GOING THE EXTRA MILE

(A SECRET THAT CAN EXPLODE YOUR SUCCESS)

"Adversity has the effect of eliciting talents which, in prosperous circumstances, would have lain dormant."

Horace

OVERVIEW

In this chapter, Hill teaches you how to make a life habit of building character, consequently making you indispensable in both relationships and the workplace.

If you've ever pondered the questions below, the answers in this chapter will surprise and inspire you:

- Why do some people succeed in life while others fail?

- Why do some people appear to be lucky, while others with equal or greater ability, training, education, brain capacity, and experience seem destined to ride with misfortune?

- Some people seem to attract success, power, and wealth with very little conscious effort. Some conquer with great difficulty, while others fail altogether to reach their ambitions, desires, and ideals. Why?

- Why do so many people work so hard and honestly without ever achieving anything in particular, while others don't seem to work hard, yet seem to get everything?

- Why are some of the smartest people among the poorest, while people of average intelligence build a fortune?

In this chapter Napoleon Hill provides the answers to these questions. When you discover the answers, your life will be altered immediately and "you will find yourself literally swept to success."

BROADCAST 2. GOING THE EXTRA MILE

ANNOUNCER:

Good afternoon, ladies and gentlemen. The famed Radio School of Success Unlimited is on the air. Napoleon Hill's Keys to Success is being brought to you in thirteen consecutive programs. Today's second lesson in the Science of Success philosophy will be given by Napoleon Hill. Time simply won't permit me to give a complete story on Mr. Hill's background. But you should know that he's the author of success books which are bestsellers in dozens of countries. Assisting Mr. Hill is Henry Alderfer, associate director of education of Napoleon Hill Institute. Now, here is Mr. Alderfer.

ALDERFER:
Good afternoon, ladies and gentlemen. This is Henry Alderfer bringing you another half-hour program featuring Napoleon Hill, the distinguished author, philosopher, and business consultant, who will discuss the philosophy of Going the Extra Mile. The idea of Going the Extra Mile means that no one ever attains outstanding success in any calling without rendering more and better service than that for which one is paid, and doing it with a pleasing, friendly mental attitude. If one works for a salary or wages, this idea should be of great benefit because it reveals the only legitimate reason one could have for asking for an increase in pay or for promotion to a better position. This is mental dynamite that may be far more explosive than the atomic bomb insofar as you can use it to blast out of your path every sort of handicap and opposition. Ladies and gentlemen, I present Napoleon Hill.

NAPOLEON HILL:
Thank you, Henry Alderfer, and good afternoon, my friends. I am especially happy to discuss the idea of Going the Extra Mile because every major benefit ever received by successful men came as the result of following the habit of making oneself useful to other people. I am profoundly impressed by the fact that more than five hundred distinguished and successful men with whom I was acquainted have attained their success very largely by adhering to the habit of Going the Extra Mile.

I will give you some examples of how this great principle works, but first I wish to emphasize this truth, that the space you occupy in your position or calling in life can be measured accurately by the quality of the service you render, plus the quantity of the service, plus the mental attitude in which you render the service. All of this, you will observe, is under your own absolute personal control.

ALDERFER:
Mr. Hill, would you mind telling us of your first discovery and use of the idea of Going the Extra Mile? I have heard you mention this, and I have never heard anything to equal it in my life.

NAPOLEON HILL:
You might say the discovery of this idea was made by sheer accident when seeking the first position I ever held. After graduation from business college it became apparent there was a lot more for me to learn than was taught in school. So I looked around and chose my desired employer with great care.

ALDERFER:
Very interesting. You chose your own employer. Isn't is customary for the employer to do the choosing?

NAPOLEON HILL:
Well, it may be customary, Henry, but I found a new and a much better way of getting the particular job I desired by following the idea of Going the Extra Mile. My choice of an employer was General Rufus A. Ayers, the most distinguished lawyer and businessman in my home state of Virginia, who owned a chain of banks, a railroad, and a number of coal mines. I decided to pitch my lot with General Ayers because of the vast knowledge that could be acquired by working under his guidance.

Here is the way I approached the general. I wrote him a letter as follows:

"Dear General Ayers,
I have just graduated from business college, and I have chosen you as my first employer. I chose you because I know I still have much to learn despite the fact that I made good grades in college, and I desire to get this training under your guidance. Therefore, I make you

the following offer: I will work for you on a three-month trial basis during which I will pay you whatever salary you think you should charge me for the training I will receive, with the understanding that at the end of the three months, if you consider I have made good, I will continue to work for you at the same salary you charged me for the first three months."

ALDERFER:
I'll risk a guess that General Ayers never received another application like yours.

NAPOLEON HILL:
No, and it is doubtful whether any other employer ever received an application like it. During these times an applicant for a position usually puts the prospective employer on the spot by wanting to know what the working hours are, how much the starting pay will be, how soon an increase can be expected, how much vacation with pay is permitted, and what extra benefits are promised.

ALDERFER:
And you might add, Mr. Hill, that oftentimes the employee not only does not go the extra mile, but he doesn't even care to go the first mile if there is any way to avoid it. You got your job with General Ayers, did you not?

NAPOLEON HILL:
Yes, I did! General Ayers did not even wait to reply by letter but called me on the telephone and said, "Come on down to my office and let me see what you look like, as I wish to make sure that you are not a visitor from Mars or some other outerworld planet." Upon arrival at the general's office, he greeted me with great enthusiasm and said, "I have just one question I wish to ask you before we begin talking about the position. Was your unusual approach in applying for a position with me your own idea, or did someone else suggest it?" When I told the general it was my own idea, he said, "That

is all I wish to know. You are employed right on the spot, and you can go to work today as a member of my secretariat at the same salary I pay all beginners."

ALDERFER:

Will you tell us what happened while you were employed by General Ayers, and especially if your unusual approach in applying for the position paid off?

NAPOLEON HILL:

Here is a brief description of what happened, and you may judge for yourself whether or not my approach based on the idea of Going the Extra Mile actually paid off. By the end of the first six months, I was promoted over six other people and was made personal secretary to General Ayers. Six months later I received another promotion—to the position of general manager of the Seaboard Coal Company, one of General Ayers's coal mine operations that employed some five hundred people. My salary was increased three times during the first year of my employment, without my asking for an increase.

ALDERFER:

In other words, you might say that your entire life's pattern was determined by one simple act of demonstrating your willingness to prove the value of your services before setting a price on them. I would say that your unusual approach in applying for a position left General Ayers little if any choice other than that of giving you a trial.

NAPOLEON HILL:

Yes, that is true; General Ayers often said the same thing. I must tell you a funny experience I had with General Ayers. One day, a client came to the office to see the general, but he was not in. The client wished to have an important legal document drawn up. Having typed a similar document for the general, I located a copy, made the necessary changes in it, and had it ready for him to inspect and approve on his return.

When he looked the document over, he called me into his office and with a broad smile on his face said, "I expect almost any day to come into this office and find you sitting at my desk." Then he became more serious and said, "Hill, there are two types of people who never get anywhere or amount to much in the world. One is the type who will not do what he is told to do, and the other is the type who will do nothing more than he is told to do. You have shown me that you are not either of these types of people."

ALDERFER:

I am also intrigued, as was General Ayers, to know just how you thought of that unusual approach in applying for a position. Would you mind giving us some information on this?

NAPOLEON HILL:

Well, Henry, there was no particular mystery about it. My common sense told me that three months of actual experience under General Ayers's guidance would be of priceless help to me in applying for a position somewhere else if the general did not wish to retain me after the three-month trial. Also, I recognized that I would gain more from three months of actual experience under a man like the general than I had gotten from my entire training in business college.

Now, Henry, I am going to tell you something that may be a surprise to you, or it may not be. You were chosen for your present position almost solely because of the very obvious fact that you understood and would follow the idea of Going the Extra Mile. There were six other applicants for the position, every one of them well qualified to fill the position, but I gave you a test, the same as I gave the others, which proved conclusively that you would be the more valuable man for the position, and you passed the test with flying colors.

ALDERFER:

I was not aware of any test. Would you mind telling me what it was?

NAPOLEON HILL:

Oh no, Henry! If I do that you might be asking for a raise in salary after this broadcast is over!

ALDERFER:

I am wondering if the dramatic method by which you contacted General Ayers for a job would be as effective today as it was then?

NAPOLEON HILL:

Henry, a sound principle never changes in effectiveness over time, and human beings and the motives by which they are influenced are the same today as they were when General Ayers was my employer. Here is a very recent experience that proves the point. Less than two months ago a man walked into an office and asked to go to work as a salesman. He believed in the product and its worth. He asked for no compensation, not even a desk, but he did ask for a list of some of the people who were interested in the company's products. He took the list, went calling on the people, and began immediately bringing in business. He made such an impressive showing that the boss had no choice but to ask him to join his staff, which he accepted under a working arrangement that may reward him very handsomely. And all this despite the fact that he was not seeking monetary benefits when he first came to work. He was seeking only an opportunity to go the extra mile, but of course he had already learned that this second mile leads directly to the end of the rainbow, where something more than a pot of gold awaits those who go there motivated by this idea.

ALDERFER:

Suppose this gentleman had come in and asked for a position in the usual manner of approach. Would he have been employed?

NAPOLEON HILL:

Frankly, no! His employer had to know something of his ability before offering him a position. But he made this unnecessary by demonstrating his ability in advance, and he did it on his own time and at his own expense.

ALDERFER:

In other words, he applied the idea of Going the Extra Mile so effectively that he actually was invited to join this staff, and on a basis that probably will pay him much more money than he would have thought of asking, had he asked to go on the payroll before demonstrating his ability. Isn't it strange why so few people learn how to get ahead in life by following the idea of Going the Extra Mile?

NAPOLEON HILL:

Yes, it is strange indeed, and you may be interested in knowing that the major reason why people are credited with being successes is the fact that they have started on the road to success by learning the benefits of Going the Extra Mile.

Here's another very interesting case where a young man lifted himself to a position of both fame and fortune by one simple act of Going the Extra Mile. It happened one frosty morning when the private railroad car of Charles M. Schwab was shifted to a side track at his employer's steel mill in Bethlehem, Pennsylvania. As Mr. Schwab climbed down from the car he was met by a young man with a notebook in his hand, who explained that he was a stenographer in the company's office and he had come down to meet Mr. Schwab with the hope that he might write any letters or telegrams that the steel master would care to send. "Who requested you to meet me here?" Mr. Schwab inquired. "It was my own idea, sir," the young man replied. "I knew you were coming in on the early-morning train because I handled the telegrams announcing your arrival."

Mr. Schwab thanked the young man for his thoughtfulness and said he would call on him later in the day if he needed his services. And he did! When the private car returned to New York City that night, young Al Williams, the stenographer who had gone the extra mile, was aboard. He was transferred, at Mr. Schwab's request, to the steel master's private office in New York. In his new job young Williams had an opportunity to meet and to become acquainted with many of Mr. Schwab's influential Wall Street banker and broker friends, and through these acquaintanceships, some five years later, he was invited to become president of a large wholesale drug company at a fabulous salary and with a stock interest in the company.

It pays to render more and better service than one is paid to render, for sooner or later it leads one to an opportunity to be paid for more than he actually does.

ALDERFER:

Do you know whether or not young Al Williams possessed other qualities than that of following the habit of Going the Extra Mile which may have contributed to his rise to fame and fortune?

NAPOLEON HILL:

I had Mr. Schwab's word for it that young Williams did not possess a single quality that entitled him to rate above the average as a stenographer, except his eagerness to be of service regardless of the pay he received or the hours he worked.

ALDERFER:

What about the many people who complain of the fact that they work for selfish people who will not recognize one's habit of Going the Extra Mile, and therefore they do not do it?

NAPOLEON HILL:

Yes, this complaint is heard many times, but this in no way changes the fact that the habit of Going the Extra Mile is the only sure way that anyone may advance himself or herself, either in business or other relationships. Ralph Waldo Emerson said, "If you serve an ungrateful master, serve him the more. Put God in your debt. Every stroke shall be repaid. The longer the payment is withholden, the better for you, for compound interest on compound interest is the rate and usage of this exchequer."

Emerson stated that by Going the Extra Mile one may put God in one's debt. This much I know—all service rendered by Going the Extra Mile comes back to one, by one means or another, and it comes back greatly multiplied. The reward does not always come back from the same source to which the service is rendered, and it often comes back from entirely unexpected sources. Croesus, the wealthy Persian philosopher, once said, "There is a wheel on which the affairs of men revolve, and its mechanism is such that it prevents any man from being always fortunate." True, there is such a wheel, but it can be made to reverse itself and turn up the winning numbers by the simple procedure of Going the Extra Mile.

ALDERFER:

Mr. Hill, can this idea of Going the Extra Mile be proved as being sound in its relationship to natural laws?

NAPOLEON HILL:

Yes, all of the principles of the success philosophy have been carefully checked and verified as being sound and in harmony with natural laws. Here's one very simple illustration that will prove to you very definitely that the idea of Going the Extra Mile is in harmony with natural laws and that it is not merely a man-made rule of conduct. Take the farmer, for example. He understands the necessity of Going the Extra Mile and follows that idea. If he didn't, the human race would perish for the lack of food. The farmer first clears his ground and gets it ready for planting. He gets no compensation for this. Then he fences his land to protect his crops. He gets no compensation for this. He plows the ground and plants it with seed. He gets no compensation for this. After this he sits down to rest and turns the job over to a higher power and waits for the seed to germinate and develop into a harvest. There would be no harvest if the farmer did not first do his part by Going the Extra Mile—in fact, many extra miles. When harvest time comes, behold, a miracle has been performed. For every grain of wheat or corn the farmer planted while Going the Extra Mile, his invisible partner gives him back a hundredfold or more than he planted. This surplus is to compensate him for his intelligence and willingness in having Gone the Extra Mile. Is this illustration clear to you, Henry?

ALDERFER:

Indeed, it is, and I am sure it is also clear to every listener to this program. It occurs to me to ask what happens to the individual who, either by ignorance or mere neglect, fails to go the extra mile, or even the first mile.

NAPOLEON HILL:

That's an interesting question and here's the answer. The person who neglects to go the first mile—the one for which he is paid—runs afoul of the law of diminishing returns and pays for his folly by the loss of his job. On the other hand, the person who faithfully follows the habit of Going the Extra Mile finds himself being pushed up the ladder of success on the wings of the law of increasing returns, which actually brings him compensation out of proportion to the service he renders. He gets the first chance at the best jobs where he works and gets top wages or better. Moreover, when business is slack and employees are laid off, he seldom, if ever, feels the axe, while others around him who do not follow the habit of Going the Extra Mile are the first to be let go. These are facts so well known to everyone that no further proof of their soundness is needed.

ALDERFER:

Mr. Hill, your statement that the reward for Going the Extra Mile does not always come back from the source to which the service is rendered intrigues me. Will you give me an illustration verifying this statement?

NAPOLEON HILL:

Yes, here is a very convincing illustration, and it is one that involves one of the most dramatic experiences of my entire career. The illustration will show that the reward that came to me for having gone the extra mile was four times removed from the act of rendering the service. The story began fifteen years ago, when I called on a friend of mine who had just opened a large cafeteria but discovered too late that he had chosen the wrong location, because when the nearby business houses closed, everyone went home, and he could not get enough dinner trade to support his cafeteria. Because of my longtime friendship with this man I offered to solve his problem by conducting a series of lectures in his cafeteria each evening. This was announced in the newspapers, and we turned away hundreds of people the first night and kept the place filled with guests every night thereafter for several weeks.

I made no charge for this service, but I did get my dinner free. Also, I had no intention of gaining any direct benefit from my service because it was a labor of love. A regular attendant at these lectures was an official of a power company who was so impressed by my interpretation of the philosophy that he invited me to address a special meeting of Southern electric power executives. Note, this was the first step in the direction of the bountiful reward I was destined to receive for Going the Extra Mile.

At the meeting of the electric power executives I was introduced to Homer Pace, vice president of the South Carolina Electric Power Company, who asked me to become acquainted with Dr. Williams P. Jacobs, a distinguished South Carolina public relations director and president of Presbyterian College, of Clinton, South Carolina. I wrote to Dr. Jacobs, and he came to Atlanta to meet me. That was step number two in the direction of my reward. Dr. Jacobs owned a large printing and publishing business, and he invited me to join him in Clinton, with the understanding that he would help me when help was needed. I accepted the invitation, and that was step number three in the direction of my reward.

After arriving in Clinton I was invited to become a faculty member of Presbyterian College, and there I gave a series of lectures. That was step number four, and the payoff came very dramatically when I became acquainted with one of the students of my class who introduced me to her sister, who is now my wife, and who has enriched my life in ways that can be evaluated only in terms of spiritual values of a most profound nature. She has brought happiness into my life that could never have been known without her influence, and it all dates back to a service I rendered to my friend with no expectation of compensation of any nature, whatsoever.

ALDERFER:

I can see from what you have just said how easy it would be for one to lose sight of the reward that comes from having Gone the Extra Mile when the receiving of the reward is several times removed from the rendering of the service. I am wondering if many people do not discount the value of the habit of Going the Extra Mile merely because the reward does not always immediately follow the rendering of the service.

NAPOLEON HILL:

Yes, many people make this mistake, and I will tell you of another equally grievous error of which some people are guilty, namely, engaging in the habit of Going the Extra Mile solely for the purpose of placing someone under obligation to them so they can claim a greater reward than they are entitled to receive.

I observed a case of this nature while I was associated with R.G. LeTourneau, as public relations counselor. This was during World War II when toolmakers were very scarce. One of Mr. LeTourneau's toolmakers came to him one day and offered to come back for two hours every evening and help out in order to keep the war materials flowing. His offer was made in such a way that he conveyed the impression he was rendering this extra service solely to help out in a crisis, and also that he would not expect pay for it. Imagine the surprise when, at the end of the first week, he presented a bill for one-and-a-half times the regular wage for this sort of work, because he worked overtime. Instead of his action lifting him in the mind of Mr. LeTourneau, it had the opposite effect, and later on, after the emergency had passed and a recommendation for an increase in the wages of the toolmakers was made, the name of this man was omitted from the increased wage list. You see, he had set into motion the law of diminishing returns, and he was later dismissed from service altogether.

ALDERFER:

Mr. Hill, I have heard that your present association with Mr. W. Clement Stone is the result of your having followed the habit of Going the Extra

Mile. Would you care to tell our radio audience the details as to how this came about?

NAPOLEON HILL:
Yes, it is true that my association with Mr. Stone came about as the direct result of having gone the extra mile. Some three years ago when in Chicago, I was invited to deliver an address before a dental association. I accepted the invitation from Dr. Everett O. Hancock, a friend of mine in Salem, Illinois, without compensation, because of this friendship. This engagement turned out to be one of the most important events of my life because Mr. Stone attended the lecture. During the luncheon preceding my lecture Mr. Stone expressed a desire to join forces with me to make success available to people throughout this and other countries.

ALDERFER:
I am beginning to catch a glimpse of something from your remarks that impresses me very much, namely, that the mental attitude in which one renders service has much to do with the effect of the service. In the two illustrations you have just mentioned of your own application of this principle, I can see that there was no element of selfishness in your action; that you served because you wished to serve and not because of expectation of any pecuniary or other form of reward.

NAPOLEON HILL:
That is correct. In closing this broadcast, I wish to give this message to men and women who work for wages or salaries. Just remember that the only possible justification for your asking for an increase in pay or a promotion to a better position is the habit of Going the Extra Mile and rendering more service and better service than you are now being paid for. It is obvious that if you are doing no more than you are now paid to do, you are already receiving all the pay to which you are entitled. To provide a sound reason for more pay you must first establish the fact that you are deserving of more pay, by Going the Extra Mile.

ALDERFER:

From the mail we have been receiving from quite a number of our listeners we find certain individuals who are interested in having their problems answered by you over the air. Are you willing to answer some of these problems for our interested listeners at the end of this broadcast?

NAPOLEON HILL:

I am glad you asked that because I have two rather interesting letters that came out of this past week's mail which I chose for this broadcast, one from Peoria and one from Milwaukee. One writer submits this problem and asks for my comments regarding it. He says, "Your Sunday broadcast brought me face to face with the weakness that has been holding me back for more than ten years. I am a salesman, and I have changed jobs on an average of once a year for these ten years. Right now I am selling life insurance, but I am not making enough to take care of my family needs. How can I increase my income and remain in the field of selling?"

My answer is gladly given with the hope that it may be helpful to many others who are engaged in selling. First of all let me point out this fact—that the big money in selling is in the training and management of salespeople, where there are scarcely any limitations to income if one is qualified to do a good job. The proper procedure for you would be to take a good course in salesmanship and condition yourself to become a teacher of salesmanship. Then organize a class and teach others to become salesmen and work under your leadership.

The inquirer from Peoria wishes to know how one can go about choosing a definite major purpose in life, and the answer to this is simple—it is a choice that every person must make for himself because no one can tell you what you should desire or what occupation you should engage in as well as you can do it for yourself. The very fact that the Creator gave you complete power to direct your mind to whatever ends you may desire naturally suggests that you should learn to use this profound privilege in all matters, and particularly in the selection of a major objective in life. Your major purpose in life should be the thing or the position or circumstance that you desire above all else. And you are the only one who can make this decision.

ALDERFER:

Listeners, you are invited to send in your questions and submit your business and personal problems for Napoleon Hill's analysis. He will select those that he believes may be representative of similar problems of other listeners to his Success School of the Air and answer as many of them as time will permit. Questions involving controversial subjects such as politics and religion will not be answered.

Next week the subject of our discussion will be the Master Mind Principle, and it will reveal to you a method by which you can become more successful than you are now by simply following its teachings. Please join us again next Sunday.

△

WISDOM TO LIVE BY

1. Either we disobey this principle of Going the Extra Mile and suffer the consequences, or we obey it and reap the rewards. It's our choice!

2. Once this principle begins to work, it piles up riches so quickly that it seems like Aladdin's lamp, drawing to one's aid an army of genies that comes laden with bags of gold.

3. The pot of gold at the end of the rainbow is not a fairy tale. The end of that Extra Mile is the spot where the rainbow ends. And that is where the pot of gold is hidden.

ADVERSITY AND ADVANTAGE

1. The story of Napoleon Hill's effort and hardship in developing the practical philosophy of success was not just built on research but experiences of real-life stresses. Hill did not receive any compensation from Andrew Carnegie and kept on going for twenty years to develop this philosophy. He endured financial hardships and continued criticism of family and friends. His entire life's pattern was determined by one simple act of demonstrating his willingness to prove the value of his services before setting a price for them. You may wonder if it paid Hill to go the extra mile for twenty years with no compensation. The answer is obvious.

2. No man is a failure who creates a single idea, much less an entire philosophy, that serves to soften the disappointments and minimize the hardship of generations to come.

3. No labor of love is ever performed at a total loss, and those who render more service and better service than what they are paid for, sooner or later receive pay for much more than they actually do.

4. If you have ever been discouraged, or if you have had difficulties to surmount that took the very soul out of you, or if you have tried and failed, then Going the Extra Mile may prove to be the "oasis in the Desert of Lost Hope for which you have been searching." As Napoleon Hill puts it, "The whole power of the Universe becomes mysteriously available" to the person who goes the extra mile.

▼

CHAPTER 3

MASTER MIND

(THE SUPREME SECRET TO ALL GREAT SUCCESSES)

△

"Achievement is not always success, while reputed failure often is. It is honest endeavor, persistent effort to do the best possible under any and all circumstances."

Orison Swett Marden

OVERVIEW

If the lack of formal schooling, education, or expertise has been a hindrance toward planning and achieving your goals, Napoleon Hill will guide you to bridge this gap.

He will also:

- Teach you how to multiply your mind power

- Make you aware of a force within you that is more powerful than the force of an atom

- Give you a formula for generating personal power to accomplish in one year what most people would achieve in their lifetime

- Show you a way to become a genius

In the following pages, you will discover how a lack of schooling or formal knowledge in planning and achieving your goal is no longer an obstacle to your success. You will be an ordinary success without the aid of others; if you want to be an outstanding success, study the text carefully, apply the principle, and you will be a great success.

BROADCAST 3. MASTER MIND PRINCIPLE

ANNOUNCER:

Good afternoon, ladies and gentlemen. The Radio School of the Air—Success Unlimited—is on the air. Napoleon Hill's famed philosophy of success is being brought to you in thirteen consecutive weekly programs. This presentation today is the third in the series. Napoleon Hill, whose success books are bestsellers all over the world, has a long and successful background. Time won't permit me to present that background now, but the School of the Air to which you are now listening follows the principles of success developed by Napoleon Hill. Assisting Mr. Hill is Henry Alderfer, associate director of education of the School of the Air. Now here is Mr. Alderfer.

ALDERFER:

Thank you. Napoleon Hill will interpret for you the magic power of the Master Mind, the success principle through which you can get the benefits of the education, the experience, and the influence of other people in carrying out your major purpose in life. The Master Mind Principle consists of the blending of two or more minds in a spirit of perfect harmony for the attainment of a definite purpose. The emphasis is on those two words, perfect harmony. He will give you convincing illustrations showing you how the Master Mind Principle has lifted individuals to great heights of personal achievement, and he will tell you that it is one of the most important factors of all great achievement. Ladies and gentlemen, here is Napoleon Hill.

NAPOLEON HILL:

Good afternoon, my friends. Perhaps Henry Alderfer's definition of the principle of the Master Mind can best be understood if you know how one man discovered this principle by sheer misfortune and used it to overcome a physical affliction that would have stopped the average man. He was a farmer who made but little more than a bare living from a small farm near Fort Atkinson, Wisconsin. When he had reached middle age, he was stricken with double paralysis and was totally disabled. As he lay in his bed he made a profound discovery. He discovered that he had a mind that had not been affected by his paralysis, and he began to explore that mind, and he discovered in it an idea that was destined to help him to convert his little farm into fabulous riches.

He called his family to his bedside and told them of his discovery and instructed them to join with him in the Master Mind alliance he needed to convert his idea into cash. He said, "I want you to plant every acre of our land in corn; then start raising hogs on the corn, and we will slaughter them while they are young and convert them into little pig sausages." That man was Milo C. Jones, and he lived to see his idea and his application of the Master Mind Principle make him a huge fortune because his Little Pig sausages became a household word all over America.

ALDERFER:

Mr. Hill, didn't Thomas A. Edison also convert a handicap into a great asset by the application of this Master Mind Principle?

NAPOLEON HILL:

Yes, after young Tom Edison had been in school only three months, his teacher sent him home with a note to his parents saying that he had an addled mind and couldn't take an education. That humiliating experience had a profound affect upon Edison, causing him to begin exploring his mind to see if he could find out what his teacher meant by the term "addled." In his search for the cause of the affliction, which had deprived him of a formal education, Edison discovered the gateway to his source of inspiration, which made him one of the greatest inventors of all time. Despite his lack of formal education, he chose an occupation where he had to make use of many of the sciences, although he knew nothing about any of them. He bridged this handicap by using the brains and the education of men who had scientific training, the same procedure used by all who achieve great success, regardless of the calling in which they may be engaged.

ALDERFER:

Mr. Hill, before you give further illustrations of successful achievement through the application of the Master Mind Principle, perhaps our audience would like you to explain the difference between this principle and ordinary coordination of effort known as cooperation.

NAPOLEON HILL:

That's a good suggestion, Henry. The major difference between the Master Mind Principle and ordinary cooperation consists of the fact that the working together of two or more minds in a spirit of perfect harmony steps up the mind power of each of the individuals to a level where the individual can draw upon the spiritual forces of the universe. Ordinary coordination of effort between individuals, which we call cooperation, doesn't lift them to this high spiritual level of thought power.

ALDERFER:

It may be helpful to our listeners if you break down this principle of the Master Mind and describe it to them step by step.

NAPOLEON HILL:

There are a number of factors by which the Master Mind Principle can be described. For example, the Master Mind Principle is the medium through which one may procure the full benefits of the experience, the training, the specialized knowledge, and the influence of other people as completely as if their minds were in reality one's own. For example, through the experience and education of a geologist, one may understand the structure of the earth without formal training in geology. Through the experience and education of the chemist, one may make practical use of chemistry, as Thomas Edison did. An active alliance of two or more minds working together for the attainment of a definite purpose stimulates each individual mind to a higher rate of vibration and conditions the mind to tune in and contact Infinite Intelligence through that state of mind known as faith.

A Master Mind alliance, properly conducted, stimulates each mind in the alliance with enthusiasm, personal initiative, imagination, and the capacity for a belief far beyond anything the individual may experience when acting alone. To be effective a Master Mind alliance must be active. The mere association of minds is not enough. They must engage in the pursuit of a definite purpose, and they must move with perfect harmony. Now do not overlook the word "perfect." Without the factor of perfect harmony, the alliance may be nothing more than ordinary cooperation, which is something vastly different from the power of the Master Mind. The Master Mind alliance gives one full access to the spiritual powers of his associates in the alliance. It is a matter of established record that all individual success where the individual has risen above mediocrity is attained by the application of the Master Mind Principle and not by individual effort alone.

ALDERFER:

I take it from what you've said, Mr. Hill, that a Master Mind in operation is something like a roundtable discussion. Most of us have observed that when a group of people begin to discuss any subject in a friendly spirit, they come up with ideas, which none of the individuals could have created by himself.

NAPOLEON HILL:

Yes, you are very close to the central core of the Master Mind Principle, but you must keep in mind the fact that a Master Mind operation also steps up the mind power of all of the individuals in the group and gives them free access to spiritual powers that are not available to them when they are acting alone. Distinguished authorities on Christianity have expressed the belief that the Nazarene and his twelve disciples constituted the first known application of the Master Mind Principle, and this explained the source of the Master's miraculous powers. Of one thing I am very sure, men and women can perform miracles through the Master Mind Principle, because it has been proven.

ALDERFER:

You have some very interesting case histories of individuals who have achieved outstanding success by applying this Master Mind Principle. Will you describe some of these for our audience?

NAPOLEON HILL:

Yes. Here's an illustration of how the Master Mind Principle, applied by a man and his wife, was responsible for the building of an industrial empire that is now worth over a billion dollars. The couple to whom I refer is Henry Ford and his wife.

ALDERFER:

How interesting. I had never heard that Mrs. Ford was actively engaged in the building of the Ford industrial empire.

NAPOLEON HILL:

She was not active as far as the public knew, but behind the scenes she was very active, and without her, Henry Ford would not have achieved the phenomenal success he did. Mrs. Ford's influence on Henry Ford first became noticeable while he was working on the first model of his automobile. He needed some parts, which were ordered from a local foundry. When he went to get the parts, he told the foundry owner that he didn't have the money to pay for them, but he would come in and pay the $30 at the end of the month. The foundry man was no fool. Or was he? For he told Ford that he couldn't get the parts until he put up the money. When Ford returned home and reported to his wife that he had been refused credit, Mrs. Ford said, "Well, Henry, we have a savings account which we have intended to use to buy a home. Go down to the bank and borrow $30 from the account." "No," said Ford. "We have promised each other we wouldn't spend that money for anything but a home." "Who said anything about spending it?" Mrs. Ford asked. "I said to go down to the bank and borrow $30 from the account. After all, we are good for the repayment of the money when you get your salary check, aren't we, Henry?"

ALDERFER:

What happened to the foundry man who refused to give Mr. Ford credit?

NAPOLEON HILL:

I met that gentleman many years later, and he told me that, as near as he could estimate, every word that he had used in turning Mr. Ford down had cost him a million dollars, because if he had placed his foundry facilities in support of Ford at that time, he could have had a substantial interest in the Ford automobile enterprise.

During Henry Ford's early days he was a shy, introverted type of man, and it was Mrs. Ford who gave him the Master Mind alliance he needed to develop the astounding courage and determination he later displayed.

ALDERFER:

I've also read that Mr. and Mrs. Thomas Edison worked together under the Master Mind Principle.

NAPOLEON HILL:

Yes, that's true, and I have heard Mrs. Edison say that no matter how late Mr. Edison remained at work in his laboratory, she always remained awake until he came home, and she discussed his day's work with him. And I heard Mr. Edison say that his wife's influence during these Master Mind discussions often led to the uncovering of facts that he had been searching for in his work.

Although it may not be generally known, there is no room for doubt that the Master Mind alliance between Abraham Lincoln and his stepmother was a strong factor in developing and revealing to the world the deep and abiding spiritual qualities that Lincoln so often drew upon throughout his life.

ALDERFER:

I get the impression from what you've said that there's some feature in the Master Mind alliance between a man and his wife which may not be present in the business or professional Master Mind alliances between men.

NAPOLEON HILL:

You are right, and the feature you refer to is the spiritual quality of love. I have noticed that wherever this relationship exists between a man and his wife, he is prosperous and successful in his business or his occupation, and also he is happy and the master of his fears and worries.

ALDERFER:

Isn't it true that our nation was conceived, born, and is now in existence as the result of the application of the Master Mind Principle?

NAPOLEON HILL:

That's absolutely true, and it is well that we remember the spirit of sacrifice and perfect harmony in which fifty-six brave men risked their lives and their fortunes when they signed the Declaration of Independence; for they well knew that this document might become their death warrant if the rebellion that followed it failed. Our great American way of life and our system of free enterprise, with all the freedom and riches these have made possible for us, are symbols of the magic power of the Master Mind.

ALDERFER:
Mr. Hill, inasmuch as you have worked very closely with two former presidents of the United States, perhaps you can describe how they applied the Master Mind Principle in the conduct of their high office.

NAPOLEON HILL:
To begin with, let me call your attention to the fact that the president and his Cabinet constitute the most powerful Master Mind alliance in existence anywhere in the world today, the purpose of which is to ensure prosperity and individual freedom to our people and, to a certain extent, the people of the entire world.

At the beginning of Franklin D. Roosevelt's first term in office, he stopped and gradually turned back the worst stampede of mass fear we've ever known by the application of this Master Mind Principle. There were a number of important people and institutions that the president used in forming his Master Mind alliance. They included the members of his own Cabinet; both Houses of Congress working in perfect harmony with the president, regardless of political affiliations; a majority of the newspapers and radio stations of the nation, which carried the presidential releases to the people; the religious leaders of the nation, regardless of their denomination; the leaders of both the major political parties; and last but not least, a majority of the people of the United States, regardless of race, creed, or political leanings. Here was an alliance of many millions of people who joined forces with the president of the United States spiritually and physically, which gave him such power as this nation had never previously witnessed, and it was sufficient to restore faith in our American way of life and our system of free enterprise, which is our economic lifeblood.

ALDERFER:

I'm sure our audience would like to know how they may get the benefit of the Master Mind Principle in attaining their aims in life.

NAPOLEON HILL:

First, adopt a definite purpose as an objective to be attained by your Master Mind alliance. Then choose individual members of the alliance whose education, experience, influence, and mental attitude are such as to make your allies of the greatest value in helping you to achieve your purpose. Third, determine what appropriate benefit each member of your Master Mind alliance shall receive in return for his activities in the alliance, remembering that no one ever does anything without an adequate motive. Fourth, establish a definite plan through which each member of the Master Mind alliance will make his contribution in working toward the achievement of the object of the alliance. Fifth, arrange a definite time and place for the discussion of operation of the plan. Keep regular means of contact between yourself and all of the members of your alliance. Sixth, it is the responsibility of the leader of a Master Mind group to see that harmony prevails among all of its members and that action is maintained constantly in carrying out the object of the alliance.

ALDERFER:

Mr. Hill, what was the most powerful Master Mind alliance you've ever known?

NAPOLEON HILL:

The alliance conducted by Franklin D. Roosevelt, which has just been described, was the most powerful I've ever known in this country, but the late Mahatma Gandhi of India had an alliance with more than 200 million of his people, which was so powerful that it enabled him to gain eventual freedom of India from British domination without the force of arms. That gives you some idea as to the power one may wield when he understands how to operate the Master Mind Principle.

The men in charge of totalitarian governments also maintained a very powerful Master Mind alliance, but they were doomed to failure because their alliance was not intended to free people but to rob them of their rights and to enslave them. The history of mankind is replete with unmistakable evidence that the Creator intended man to be a free agent, to live his own life in his own way. The best proof of that is the fact that no self-appointed world conqueror has ever lived to see his ambition fulfilled. Remember that any acts of human beings, whether by individuals or groups of individuals, that are not in harmony with the overall plan of the universe must ultimately end in failure.

ALDERFER:
Mr. Hill, where is there the greatest opportunity for men and women to benefit by the application of this Master Mind Principle?

NAPOLEON HILL:
The place where the Master Mind is needed most is in the home, where it should be the means of knitting together the relationship between man and wife and every other member of the family. There is always prosperity and happiness in homes where this principle is followed faithfully. Homes, like people, have individual personalities that reflect the mental attitude and the relationship of the people who live in them. Wherever the Master Mind relationship prevails in a home, the place vibrates with happiness and success that inspires every member of the family.

ALDERFER:
Is this not true of places of business also?

NAPOLEON HILL:
Yes, and there are many people who are so sensitive to the environmental vibrations of places of business that they can recognize instantly when they walk into a place of business what sort of people do business there. Ralph Waldo Emerson said, "Every business is the extended shadow of

one man." And that extended shadow, whether it is negative or positive, is nothing but the sum total of the sort of thinking this one man inspires in his fellow workers. If Emerson were speaking today he would have to change the wording of his statement by saying that every business is the extended shadow of one man or one woman, for it is true that women are taking their places alongside of men in this modern age of equal privileges for all.

ALDERFER:

Mr. Hill, aren't there some references in the Bible that clearly indicate that the blending of two or more minds in a spirit of harmony may be the key that opens the door to the limitless power of the universal mind?

NAPOLEON HILL:

Yes, in the Bible there is a passage: Matthew eighteenth chapter, nineteenth verse: If two of you shall agree here on earth concerning anything that you shall ask, it shall be done for you by my father which is in heaven. Also, there are other references in the Bible that would lead one to the conclusion that the Master Mind Principle has most profound connotations in connection with the powers of prayer.

ALDERFER:

What happens in a business or any other organization where the owners or principals neglect to relate themselves to their associates under this Master Mind Principle?

NAPOLEON HILL:

I suppose you ask that question in order to emphasize a point, because you know that friction at the top levels of management breaks up more businesses than all other causes combined. R. G. LeTourneau has said that friction in the machinery of his four large industrial plants cost him millions of dollars annually, but that was nothing in comparison with the cost of friction in the relationship between employees. We might go a step further and quote another great industrialist who recently said that the friction between management and labor leaders, if it continues in its present trend, might well be the means of destroying the entire American system of free enterprise.

ALDERFER:

Is the cost of friction in human relations measurable only in terms of monetary costs, or are there other factors that affect individuals who do not relate themselves to one another harmoniously?

NAPOLEON HILL:

Peace of mind and mental attitude are affected by friction in human relations. It is well nigh impossible for anyone who is not happy to maintain sound health. Distinguished doctors say that stomach ulcers are the result of troubled minds, so you see that the cost of friction in human relations is measurable in things that cannot be evaluated in terms of money. Moreover, the person who goes to prayer with a mind filled with hatred and fear and envy and doubt always comes away empty-handed. Therefore, it is obvious that the Master Mind Principle based upon harmony and friendly coordination of effort between people is the most important factor in human relations.

ALDERFER:

I'm beginning to see now why you so strongly advocate the adoption of the Master Mind relationship between married people. Because it is obvious from what you have said, that even the family prayers are not effective where harmony and peace of mind do not prevail in the family relationship.

Now we come to answering the questions you, our listeners, have submitted by mail, inspired by previous broadcasts. Napoleon Hill will select the questions to be answered on this program each week. The first question for today, Mr. Hill, comes from Indianapolis and the writer is a gentleman who says, "I am employed in a position where I am not permitted to go the extra mile, and if I did so, I would be fired. How can I overcome this problem?" What's your answer?

NAPOLEON HILL:

You owe it to yourself to find a position where you can exercise the privilege of advancing yourself by increasing the quantity and the quality of the service you render. Obviously, you should find another position where you will be rewarded, not penalized, for going the extra mile, because that is the only way you can promote yourself to a better way of living.

ALDERFER:

The next question comes from a mechanic in Milwaukee. He says, "I have perfected a device to be attached to a carburetor that will save up to 10 percent of the gasoline used in an automobile. I have had this device in operation on my car for six months and it works perfectly. How can I get it protected and marketed?"

NAPOLEON HILL:

The first thing you should do is go see a patent attorney and let him procure a patent for you, if your device is entirely new. After you get your patent, or while your application for a patent is pending, see if you can find a local manufacturer who will produce and market your device on a royalty basis. Do not undertake to manufacture or market your device by yourself, but leave this to experienced businessmen who have the know-how and the capital to do the job right.

ANNOUNCER:

Thank you, Mr. Hill. We have run out of time this afternoon. Ladies and gentlemen, you have just heard Napoleon Hill, the man who gave the world its first practical philosophy of personal achievement. As Mr. Hill has said, the purpose of the Success School of the Air is to inspire people with ideas they can use in promoting themselves into greater success. Please tune in again next Sunday, when Mr. Hill will discuss the three major causes of failure.

WISDOM TO LIVE BY

1. An all-wise Providence has so arranged the mechanism of the mind that no single mind is complete. Richness of the mind, in its fullest sense, comes from the harmonious alliance of two or more minds, working toward the achievement of some definite purpose.

2. Psychologists say that no two minds ever come into contact without there being born of that association a third and intangible mind, of greater power than either of the two minds. This is as immutable as the law of gravity, which holds the stars and planets in their places.

3. Nothing short of miraculous is the power of the human mind when united with other minds in harmony and with a definite purpose.

4. The Master Mind is the highest form of creative effort now known to mankind, and its potential staggers the imagination.

5. Perhaps in the Master Mind lies the answer to problems of world peace and other difficulties that beset humanity.

ADVERSITY AND ADVANTAGE

1. The Master Mind alliance creates a state of mind that enables you to meet danger and difficulties with firmness, resolution, and valor. It is really a form of mental power that comes from self-confidence and success consciousness.

2. A group of storage batteries will provide more energy than a single battery. This comparison holds true with the mind and leads to the important conclusion that a group of minds coordinated in the spirit of harmony will provide more thought energy than a single mind to face any difficulty or challenge.

CHAPTER 4

THE THREE MAJOR CAUSES OF FAILURE

(OUR GREATEST BLESSING MAY BE OUR GREATEST SORROW)

"Failure is nothing more than a kindly, unseen hand that halts you on your chosen course and with great wisdom forces you to redirect your efforts along more advantageous pathways."

Napoleon Hill

OVERVIEW

Have you ever wondered why some people, when confronted with adversity or defeat, simply crumble and become victims, while others are strengthened?

In this lesson, you learn that every defeat, every disappointment, and every adversity carry with it a seed of equivalent or greater benefit. You will discover answers to these important questions:

- Why is failure a temporary defeat and usually a blessing in disguise?

- Why is defeat a destructive force only when you accept it?

- How do failures guide you to finding what you truly love?

With the knowledge and concepts in this chapter, your new attitude toward defeat may prove to be a real turning point in your life.

BROADCAST 4. THE THREE MAJOR CAUSES OF FAILURE

ANNOUNCER:
The Success Unlimited School is on the air, presenting Napoleon Hill, who will bring you another dynamic program that may start you on your way to a more prosperous and better way of living. Napoleon Hill is said to have made more successful men and women than has any other living person, and his success books are bestsellers in every country on earth. In today's program Mr. Hill will describe for you the three major causes of failure. Associated with Mr. Hill on today's program is Henry Alderfer, the associate director of education of the Napoleon Hill Institute. Mr. Alderfer.

ALDERFER:
Mr. Hill, inasmuch as our Success School of the Air is presenting a success formula that people can live by, at their work and play, in their jobs and homes, you have been and will be describing the success principles that must

be followed by our listeners. While you are telling our audience what they must do in order to achieve success, will you also tell our friends what they must not do?

NAPOLEON HILL:

Yes! And we'll begin our program today by describing the three most common causes of failure. You will observe that all three of these stumbling blocks can be converted into stepping-stones to success by following the rules presented through these Success School of the Air programs.

Cause of failure number one: Inability to get along with other people. Regardless of how well educated you may be, or how responsible your job may be, or how much money you may have, if you cannot induce people to like you, if you cannot get along with all sorts of people under all circumstances, you can never become a great success in any undertaking. The first step you must take in causing people to like you is to begin liking them and expressing it in the tone of your voice, a pleasant smile when you are speaking to others, and a sincere desire to be helpful to others whether they deserve it or not.

Cause of failure number two: The habit of quitting when the going is hard. No matter who you are or how skilled you may be in your occupation, there will be times when the going is hard, and unpleasant circumstances will overtake you and make you want to give up. If you yield easily to these obstacles you may as well write yourself off as far as becoming a great success is concerned. But, assuming that you will follow the success rules presented on this program, when you meet with opposition of any nature, instead of quitting you will turn on more willpower, kindle the fires of a stronger faith in your own ability, and make up your mind that, come what may, you will not sell yourself short.

I had one of the greatest thrills of my life when Thomas Edison told me how he reacted to failure while he was trying to perfect the incandescent electric lamp. Before he found the solution to his problem, he tried more than ten thousand different ideas, every one of which was a failure. Think of it! A man keeping on through ten thousand failures with faith unshaken, and at long last crowned with victory. One failure is sufficient to make the average person quit. Perhaps this is why there are so many average persons and only one Thomas Edison.

Cause of failure number three: Procrastination—inability to make prompt and definite decisions. The habit of waiting for something beneficial to happen instead of getting busy and making something happen. All successful people in the higher brackets of life make it their habit to create circumstances and opportunities favorable to themselves instead of accepting whatever life offers them.

ALDERFER:
Could you tell us what happens to the person who fails to move on his own initiative and embrace opportunity when it presents itself?

NAPOLEON HILL:
Yes, I can give you a wonderful illustration of the costliness of indecision and procrastination. Some years ago one of the large automobile manufacturing companies decided to begin an extensive expansion program. The company president called in one hundred young men from the various departments of the plant and said to them, "Gentlemen, we are going to enlarge our plant and greatly increase our output of automobiles, which means that we will need executives and department managers far beyond our present staff. We are offering each of you young men the privilege of working four hours per day in the office, where you will learn to become executives, and four hours at your regular jobs in the plant. There will be some homework you must do at night, and there may be times when you will have to forego your social duties and work overtime. Your pay will be the same that you are now getting in the plant. I am passing out cards on which I wish each of you who will accept our offer to write your name, and I will give you one hour in which to talk among yourselves and make up your minds."

ALDERFER:
Of course all of them accepted the opportunity?

NAPOLEON HILL:

No! When the president of the company picked up the cards he got one of the biggest surprises of his life. Only twenty-three out of the one hundred accepted the offer. But, the next day thirty more of the men came into the president's office and informed him they had made up their minds to accept, some of them explaining that they had reached a decision to accept after talking the matter over with their wives.

ALDERFER:

What happened to these thirty?

NAPOLEON HILL:

The president said, "Gentlemen, you were given one hour in which to consider the offer and make up your minds. I'm sorry, but this opportunity is gone forever, because I have learned from experience that the man who cannot or will not make up his mind quickly and definitely when he has all the necessary facts to enable him to do so will change his mind quickly at the first sign of obstacles; or he will allow other people to talk him into changing his mind."

ALDERFER:

Mr. Hill, you have a remarkable story in your relationship with Andrew Carnegie that shows what promptness of decision can do to seize upon favorable opportunities. I'm sure our audience would like you to describe your experience, which was destined to benefit not only yourself, but millions of men and women throughout the world.

NAPOLEON HILL:

The experience you mentioned happened over forty years ago, when I first met Andrew Carnegie, the great industrialist who founded the United States Steel Corporation. I went to see Mr. Carnegie to write a success story for a magazine based on his stupendous achievements. Originally he allotted me three hours for the interview, but actually it lasted three days and nights, during which he was also interviewing me, with a purpose in mind, without my knowing what he was up to. During those three days he was telling me that the world needed a new success philosophy, organized and written down, that would give the average man or woman the full benefit of all that he and other successful men like himself had learned from a lifetime of experience. He said it was a sin of major proportions that successful men allowed their hard-earned experience to be buried with their bones.

At the end of the third day Mr. Carnegie said, "I have been talking to you for three days about the need for a practical success philosophy. Now I'm going to ask you one question that I want you to answer with a simple yes or no, but don't answer until you make up your mind definitely. If I commission you to organize the world's first practical success philosophy, will you devote twenty years to research, and to interviewing successful people, and earn your own way as you go along, without a financial subsidy from me? Yes or no.

ALDERFER:

Of course, you told him yes, because if you had not done so, we would not be here on this program today, would we?

NAPOLEON HILL:

I said, "Yes, Mr. Carnegie, I'll accept your offer, and you may depend upon it that I will carry out the assignment." Mr. Carnegie said, "All right—you have the job—and I like the mental attitude in which you accepted the assignment." I learned some years later that Mr. Carnegie was holding a stopwatch behind his desk, and he had allotted me exactly sixty seconds in which to make up my mind, after he had given me three whole days in which to get the facts.

ALDERFER:

How many of those precious seconds had you used up before you gave your answer?

NAPOLEON HILL:

Exactly twenty-nine seconds. That left a margin of thirty-one seconds between me and an opportunity such as probably no other author ever received. I learned later that Mr. Carnegie had given more than 250 people the same test he gave me, and every one of them flunked it because of failure to make up his mind promptly. Mr. Carnegie said that the time required by most of those 250 to make up their minds ran all the way from three hours to three years.

ALDERFER:

Why did Mr. Carnegie place so much emphasis on the matter of prompt decision?

NAPOLEON HILL:

He explained that no one can be counted upon to carry our important assignments or to assume important responsibilities without following the habit of quick and definite decisions. In my case, Mr. Carnegie was also searching for another quality without which he knew I would never follow through with the twenty years of research that were necessary in order to find out what makes successful men and women.

ALDERFER:

What quality was that?

NAPOLEON HILL:

It was the habit of turning on more willpower instead of quitting when the going is hard. Mr. Carnegie knew that there is always a time in every undertaking when one meets with obstacles and may be overtaken by opposition, and he recognized that the quitter never wins, and the winner never quits.

ALDERFER:

What was your greatest obstacle while you were doing the twenty years of research in organizing the success philosophy that has made you famous throughout the world?

NAPOLEON HILL:

My greatest obstacle was friends and relatives who believed I had undertaken too big a job. And they chided me for working for the richest man in the world for twenty years without financial compensation from him. One of the queer traits of most people, especially one's own relatives, is that they so often discourage any member of the family who steps out ahead of the crowd and aspires to achieve outstanding success.

ALDERFER:

How did you manage to keep up your spirits and sustain your faith for so long a time in the face of opposition from your relatives?

NAPOLEON HILL:

I didn't do it alone. I had help through a Master Mind alliance with two people who gave me encouragement when the going was tough. These were Mr. Carnegie, my sponsor, and my stepmother who was the only member of my family who believed I would endure through twenty years of rough going. One of the great miracles in human relations consists in the power of survival, which one may acquire by a friendly alliance with one or more other persons.

ALDERFER:

Did you get help from other successful men besides Mr. Carnegie while you were organizing the philosophy of success?

NAPOLEON HILL:

Oh yes! And if I hadn't, we would not be here on this program today. There was scarcely a single person of outstanding achievements during my association with Mr. Carnegie who did not cooperate with me by supplying a portion of that which went into the making of the science of success. But I learned one very interesting fact about people while I was struggling to complete my work and receive recognition for it. I learned that when one needs anything very badly, it is difficult for him to find anyone who wishes to help him get it. But, when one gets over the hump, achieves recognition and money, and no longer needs help, then just about everybody wants to do something for him.

ALDERFER:
Isn't there something in the Bible that corroborates what you have just said?

NAPOLEON HILL:
Yes, there is, and while I will not undertake to quote it verbatim, it goes something like this: "To him that hath it shall be given, and to him that hath not, it shall be taken away, even unto that which he hath."—The first time I read this passage in the Bible I questioned the soundness of it, but the sober experiences of my later years proved conclusively that this is a trait of mankind. No one wants to be associated with or to help a failure, while almost everyone will go out of their way to help one who does not need help. This is explained by the law through which like attracts like.

Now let me call your attention to the fact that every failure, every adversity, and every unpleasant circumstance carry with it the seed of an equivalent benefit or advantage. The person who has a sound philosophy to live by learns quickly how to find this seed of equivalent benefit and to germinate it into an advantage. As far as luck is concerned, it may be true that it often does play a temporary part in the lives of people. But remember this truth—if luck brings temporary defeat or failure, one does not have to accept this as permanent—and, by searching for that seed of an equivalent benefit, one may actually transform a failure into enduring success.

ALDERFER:
Could you give me an example illustrating your point that adversity carries with it the seed of an equivalent benefit?

NAPOLEON HILL:
Yes, there are hundreds of examples I could relate if time permitted, but I will give you two, one of which changed the entire course of my life, and,

through my efforts it has changed the lives of many people. My mother passed away when I was only eight years old. To most people, that of course would seem like an irreparable loss, but the seed of an equivalent benefit that came from my loss was found in a wise and understanding stepmother, who took my own mother's place and was destined to inspire me with courage and faith when I most needed these.

The other example is that of Abraham Lincoln's great sorrow over the loss of his first love, through the death of Ann Rutledge. That experience reached deeply into the spiritual forces of the great Lincoln's soul and revealed to the world the qualities that were destined to make him one of our greatest presidents in the time of our greatest need. You might say it was bad luck or misfortune that deprived Lincoln of the woman of his first love, but it was Mr. Lincoln's reaction and adjustment to this loss that revealed the greatness of his soul. Rather than despairing, he redoubled his efforts to educate himself and to persevere and excel in his chosen callings.

No human experience should ever be charged off as a complete loss, because every circumstance of our lives, whether pleasant or unpleasant, places us in the way of learning how to live and how to get along with other people.

ALDERFER:
During your contacts with Thomas Edison, did you get the impression that he was handicapped by his deafness?

NAPOLEON HILL:
On the contrary. Much to my surprise, I discovered that Mr. Edison's deafness was a blessing instead of a curse, because he found the seed of an equivalent benefit that his deafness yielded, and made astounding use of that seed. Once I asked Mr. Edison if his deafness were not a handicap and he said, "No, it is a blessing because it has taught me to hear from within."

ALDERFER:
Just what did Mr. Edison mean by that response?

NAPOLEON HILL:

He meant that his deafness had caused him to develop his sixth sense, through which he learned how to tune in and make contact with sources of knowledge outside of those available through the five physical senses. It was from these outside sources that he got much of the knowledge that made him the greatest inventor of all time. And while I am on this subject, may I tell you that throughout the twenty years I spent in analyzing successful people to learn what made them tick, I discovered that successful people almost invariably were successful in almost exact proportion to the extent that they had met and mastered obstacles and defeat.

ALDERFER:

How do you explain this?

NAPOLEON HILL:

It can be explained by considering that Nature has so arranged the affairs of men that strength grows out of struggle. If men had no problems and were never forced to exert themselves, they would atrophy and wither away through disuse of their brain cells, the same as would happen with an arm or a leg if it were not given exercise. Nature penalizes people who neglect to properly use their physical bodies. The same is true of the brain cells with which we think. If we do not use the mind, it becomes lazy and unreliable.

Human problems force people to develop their minds through use, to think, to reason, to imagine, and to solve problems. Look what happens to the children of very wealthy people who allow their offspring to grow up under the delusion that because their parents have money they do not have to work or to prepare themselves to live on their own initiative. Rarely does such a person become fully independent or self-determining.

ALDERFER:

You had some experiences with struggle on your own account during your early days, did you not?

NAPOLEON HILL:

Yes, I was blessed at birth with four powerful causes for struggle, namely, poverty, fear, superstition, and illiteracy.

ALDERFER:

Did you say blessings?

NAPOLEON HILL:

Yes, blessings, because I was destined to devote my life to helping my fellow man overcome these four common causes of failure, and I needed to learn something about them at their source.

On the lighter side of my blessings, you may be interested in knowing that I was tagged with the name Napoleon because of the hope of my parents that a great uncle by the same name would leave me a portion of his fortune when he died. But, fortunately, he did not! I say fortunately because I know what happened to those to whom he did leave his money! It was soon squandered, while I, in my struggle to overcome poverty, fear, superstition, and illiteracy, uncovered knowledge that I have been privileged to share with millions of people who have benefitted by it.

ALDERFER:

If you had a friend or a son or a student who was preparing to make his own way in the world, and you had to select some one trait on which you would urge him to depend most for success, what would this trait be?

NAPOLEON HILL:

That is a sixty-four-dollar question but, without hesitation, I'll say that I would select that trait which inspires or compels a person to keep on going when the going is hard instead of giving up and quitting. I would select this trait because it is the one that has served me at times when my future seemed hopeless by any standard of evaluation. And I would select it because I have never seen or heard of anyone who achieved success above mediocrity without this trait. I would select it also because I have reason to believe that the Creator intended people to become wise and strong through struggle.

ALDERFER:
Your remarks about the sons of very rich men prompt me to ask if, during your contacts with wealthy Americans, you discovered any son of a rich man who equaled or excelled his father in business or otherwise?

NAPOLEON HILL:
Only one! And that was John D. Rockefeller Jr., who not only caught up with the achievements of his father, but to my way of thinking excelled his father in many respects. Poverty is often a great curse, but only because people accept it as such and not as an inspiration to render the sort of service that can master poverty. Inherited wealth is often a great curse as well.

ALDERFER:
From what you've been saying I judge that you believe a poor man's son has a much better chance of success than the son of a rich man.

NAPOLEON HILL:
All of my observations during the past forty-odd years convince me conclusively that the poor man's son has the better chance, provided that he does not accept poverty as something he has to tolerate, but instead makes up his mind to master it.

ALDERFER:
What was your first reaction to Andrew Carnegie's offer to sponsor you to write a philosophy of success on condition that you earn your own way, without a cash subsidy from him?

NAPOLEON HILL:
My first reaction was the same as that which most anyone would have experienced. I believed his requirements were unfair in view of his great

wealth, but I learned later that this was one of the shrewdest moves that Mr. Carnegie ever made in his relations with me, because it forced me to become resourceful and to learn how to apply the principles of success in sustaining myself while engaged in the financially unprofitable work of research into the causes of success. Because of this foresight on the part of Mr. Carnegie I lived to see the day, and not too far from my beginning with him, when I did not need his financial help.

ALDERFER:

Many of our friends would be interested in knowing how you managed to support yourself during the twenty years of research you devoted to your work before it became remunerative.

NAPOLEON HILL:

I have been asked that same question many times. I was an experienced newspaperman when I first met Mr. Carnegie, and my work in this field sustained me for a time. Later I began to train men and women in salesmanship; and it turned out that I had talent in this field. During my work in the field of salesmanship I trained over thirty thousand people, many of whom became master salesmen.

ALDERFER:

Just one more personal question, and I'll let you off the hook! How do you manage to stay so energetic and active and young at the age of seventy-one?

NAPOLEON HILL:

I remain young by keeping busy in a labor of love, and by the habit of celebrating every birthday by taking off a year from my age instead of adding one. I am now back in my late thirties! But, perhaps, to speak more seriously, I close each day's labor with a prayer that keeps my store of blessings eternally filled, and I shall express that prayer now—"Oh Infinite Intelligence, I ask not for more riches, but for more wisdom with which to make better use of the blessings with which I was endowed at birth, through the privilege of embracing my own mind and directing it to ends of my own choice. Amen."

ALDERFER:

Mr. Hill, the time has come for you to answer a few of the many questions that have come into our office in reference to problems that have arisen in the minds of individuals in our radio audience. Will you give our listeners the benefit of your wise counsel in answering some of them?

The first one comes from a woman who says, "I am secretary to a man who believes that a woman is not entitled to promotion to an executive job. I have the ability to fill a much more responsible position than I now have. How should I go about getting the position?"

NAPOLEON HILL:

I would suggest that you manage to get permission to do some of the work connected with the higher position and that you do it on your own time, and gratuitously. It is not likely that your employer would object to your working overtime without pay, and by doing so, you will prove your ability to fill the better position.

ALDERFER:

The next one comes from a man who desires to go into business for himself. He says, "I work for a large trucking company, and I know its business from top to bottom. I wish to start a trucking business of my own, but I do not have the capital with which to buy the necessary equipment. How would you suggest that I get the necessary money?"

NAPOLEON HILL:

You should advertise for a partner who would be willing to lend you the necessary capital and who would also take over a portion of the responsibilities of the business. In this way you would invest your experience against the other fellow's money and the arrangement should be satisfactory to both of you if you get the right man. Try an advertisement in the financial section of the Sunday *Chicago Tribune* and in the *Wall Street Journal*, and you will likely find the man you need.

ALDERFER:

Here is one from a young man who is about to finish high school. He says, "I will be graduated this year, and I wish to get a position with some able businessman so I may get the benefit of his experience. What should I do to get such a position?"

NAPOLEON HILL:

One approach would be for you to take a business college course—unless you can get business training in high school—and prepare yourself as a secretary. Competent secretaries are exceedingly hard to find, and you would have no trouble locating a position. Also, you could practically be sure of choosing your own employer. In a job of this sort you would have access to business contacts and the benefit of experience of a successful businessman, which would be of priceless value to you as a stepping-stone to something better.

ALDERFER:

A college professor says, "A growing family makes it necessary for me to earn more money than my present position as a teacher now pays or will ever pay. What should I do about this?"

NAPOLEON HILL:

The answer is obvious. Get into some other field of endeavor such as selling, for example. You could make the break from your present work by starting as a part-time salesman, working during evenings, until you prove to yourself that you can sell.

ALDERFER:

Thank you for your counsel to these problems.

ANNOUNCER:

Thank you, Napoleon Hill, and thank you to our audience for tuning in to this afternoon's broadcast. Please join us again next Sunday when Mr. Hill will tell you how to condition your mind for success.

△

WISDOM TO LIVE BY

1. Napoleon Hill has given a new meaning to failure. If we look at failure as a temporary defeat and a blessing in disguise, our attitude toward defeat becomes more positive.

2. Education, skills, and experience are useful assets in every calling, but they will be of little value to the person who gives up when defeated.

3. When defeat overtakes you, don't spend all your time counting your losses. Save some of your time to count the gains, and you may find they are greater than your losses.

4. Adversity shows what you are made of; it brings out your finest qualities.

5. Loss of material things can help you discover an intangible fortune of such magnitude that it cannot be measured in material terms.

6. Pain, setbacks, defeats, disgrace, and losses are the misfortune we all must suffer, for they are simply a part of the human condition!

7. No one wins all the time.

8. No human experience should ever be written off as a complete loss, because every circumstance of our lives, whether pleasant or unpleasant, places us in the way of learning how to live.

ADVERSITY AND ADVANTAGE

1. Failure and adversity have introduced many people to opportunities that they would not have recognized under more favorable circumstances.

2. The most important moment in your life is when you recognize that you have met with defeat. It is the most important because it provides you with dependable means to foretell the possibilities of your future success.

3. If you accept defeat as an inspiration to try again with renewed confidence and determination, the attainment of your success will be only a matter of time. If you accept defeat as final and allow it to destroy your confidence, you may as well abandon your hope of success. Every defeat will mark an important turning point in your life.

▼

CHAPTER 5

HOW TO CONDITION YOUR MIND FOR SUCCESS

(A WAY TO INFLUENCE YOUR LUCK, FATE, CHANCE, AND DESTINY)

OVERVIEW

In this chapter, Hill's purpose is to move you from failure consciousness to success consciousness.

You will learn about:

- The system within you that you are constantly using to your disadvantage

- How this system has a power to restrain all the evil forces such as poverty, fear, ill health, and hatred from your life

- How this system is also a cure for friction in human relationships and can bring harmony and peace to your life

- Why it is essential to guard this system to protect you from all adversities

With the knowledge gleaned from this chapter, you will be well on your way to using the power of this system to take control of your life.

BROADCAST 5. HOW TO CONDITION YOUR MIND FOR SUCCESS

ANNOUNCER:

Success Unlimited is on the air, presenting once more the distinguished philosopher Napoleon Hill, whose success books have benefitted millions of people throughout the world. You are going to have a treat in today's program when Napoleon Hill gives you a brand-new system for the development of a success consciousness and tells you how you can use this system to bring you riches and all of life's values that you most desire. Assisting Mr. Hill is Henry Alderfer, associate director of education of the Napoleon Hill Institute. Mr. Alderfer.

ALDERFER:

Thank you, and I want to alert our audience to be ready today for an entirely new approach to your personal success based on mind-conditioning principles that may be entirely new to you. Listen carefully and keep an open mind, because the message you are about to hear may mark the most important change in your entire life if you are ready for a better and more abundant way of life. Now here is Napoleon Hill, who has proved the soundness of the principles he is going to pass on to you by making them bring him success on his own terms. Mr. Hill.

NAPOLEON HILL:
Good afternoon, my radio friends. May I begin by calling your attention to the fact that this world in which you and I live—and struggle—and stumble and fall—then arise again in our efforts to find our rightful places—confronts us with two powerful forces we must deal with? One is the force of good, and the other is the force of evil. Perhaps you might prefer to identify these two forces as God and the Devil, but regardless of the names you give them, we know they are very real powers that affect the lives of all of us for weal or for woe. Because I have been blessed with the privilege of learning a system by which the evil force can be restrained, I feel it my duty and privilege to pass it on to you and all others who may be ready to receive it.

ALDERFER:
Mr. Hill, does the system give one immunity against all of the evil forces that get in the way of people who are trying to live right and find happiness and prosperity, such forces as poverty, fear, ill health, and hatred?

NAPOLEON HILL:
Yes, it has given me complete immunity against all of these forces, and it has done the same for many thousands of others. The system embraces the same fundamental principle that Emil Coué prescribed so successfully more than thirty years ago. Coué reduced the formula to its simplest terms by teaching his followers to improve themselves with this short sentence, "Day by day, in every way, I am getting better and better."

ALDERFER:

Of course Coué was teaching people how to make use of autosuggestion as a means of keeping their minds positive, was he not?

NAPOLEON HILL:

Precisely, and it is important to remember that many of us are using autosuggestion every day, not to combat the evil forces but instead to give them an open door to come in and bring us misery. This is borne out by the fact that the majority of people go through life plagued by frustrations, failures, and poverty because they allow their minds to dwell upon these undesirable things. It is a known fact that the mind attracts the physical equivalent of that which it feeds upon.

ALDERFER:

It is obvious, then, that a mind-conditioning system is designed to teach people how to use the power of autosuggestion to condition the mind with a success consciousness so as to get the things they desire, and not the things they do not desire.

NAPOLEON HILL:

You couldn't have stated it better, Henry. The system gives one a controlled way of living and a method for keeping the mind attuned to the forces of good and protected against the forces of evil of every nature whatsoever. All thoughts—both the positive and the negative—attract the people and the things that are akin to them.

ALDERFER:

This being true, it is quite obvious that one should have a means of controlling the thoughts on which the subconscious mind acts, since it will accept and act upon fear just as readily as it will accept and act upon faith.

NAPOLEON HILL:

That is true, and right here let us take notice of the most profound fact by which people may direct and to a great extent control their earthly destinies, namely, that the Creator gives every individual complete, absolute, and unchallengeable control over but one thing, the privilege of control of the power of thought. You can let your mind think in terms of misery and failure and poverty, and these undesirable things will be attracted to you as surely as night follows day. On the other hand, you can deliberately plan and direct your mind to dwell on opulence, happiness, and success, and it will just as unerringly attract these desirable things to you.

Isn't it logical to assume that by giving man control over but one thing the Creator intended this to be the most important thing available to man? One thing stood out profoundly in the lives of every one of the successful people I have ever known, and this was the fact that each of them had a system for controlling his mind and keeping it busily engaged with circumstances and things that were desired—things that represented success. I have also noticed, by observing thousands of failures, that not one of them had a system for controlling and directing his mind to definite ends, but instead they drifted aimlessly with the uncertainties of chance.

ALDERFER:
I know you have a system for controlling and directing the mind that works, and I know our radio friends are anxiously awaiting your description of it.

NAPOLEON HILL:
Yes, I do have a workable system, and I am happy to share it with all who are ready to accept it and put it to work. The system consists of what I am pleased to call my Guiding Princes. There are nine of these invisible servants, each of whom has been assigned a definite job to do on my behalf. The combined responsibility of the nine princes is that of giving me a well-rounded and properly balanced life suited to the carrying out of my major purpose in life, which is that of helping people to take possession of their own minds.

ALDERFER:

I am sure our radio friends would like you to describe each of the Guiding Princes and tell what particular service each performs on your behalf. Also, how you manage to keep the princes constantly engaged in your service, what compensation you offer them, etc.

NAPOLEON HILL:

In describing the princes I will present them in the order that I communicate with them many times daily for the purpose of expressing my gratitude for the services they render me, beginning with The Prince of Sound Health.

It is this prince's responsibility to vitalize every individual cell and individual organ of my body, and to keep my physical body continually free from unfriendly elements so that I may enjoy perfect health. It is also the duty of this prince to give me the wisdom with which to cooperate intelligently in doing my part to keep my body healthy and efficient.

The Prince of Prosperity is charged with the responsibility of keeping me supplied with every material substance I desire or need, including money, from sources where I have earned the right to have these blessings, and it is the responsibility of this prince to give me the wisdom with which to use wisely all riches of every nature that I may receive.

The Prince of Peace of Mind is charged with the responsibility of keeping my mind free from the causes of fear and worry and of keeping my mind always open and free from intolerance of every nature. This prince also screens my mind against the encroachment of all thoughts and forces except those that I invite.

The Prince of Hope reveals to me images of the future that inspire and aid me in the daily performance of my duties, and that give me the courage to make beginnings before I can foresee the endings in my chosen field of labor.

The Prince of Faith keeps the passageway between my mind and Infinite Intelligence constantly open and protects me against the acceptance of unnecessary limitations and negative thoughts in the performance of my duties. This prince also inspires me to undertake and to successfully complete aims and purposes that many people would regard as impossible of attainment.

The Prince of Love keeps me eternally youthful in both body and mind and relates me to my fellow man in a spirit of understanding, which gives me a wide latitude of opportunity to be of service to people of all races and all creeds.

The Prince of Romance makes all of my tasks and activities a labor of love and keeps me eternally alerted to the truth that no human experience is ever wasted or lost, except by one's negative mental attitude toward it.

The Prince of Patience gives me the self-discipline I need in order to adjust myself in all my human relationships so that I may deal justly and fairly with everyone under all circumstances. It also keeps me reminded that time and the proper timing of my acts and deeds can solve problems that yield to nothing else.

The Prince of Overall Wisdom keeps the other eight princes eternally active on my behalf, while I sleep as well as when I am awake, and so relates me to every circumstance which touches my life, that I benefit by it whether the circumstance be pleasant or unpleasant. And this prince reveals to me the seed of an equivalent advantage that exists in connection with every adversity I may encounter.

There you have a description of my little army of invisible servants through whom I avail myself of that profound privilege granted to me by my Creator to take full possession of my own mind and direct it to ends of my own choice.

ALDERFER:
Do you give verbal orders to your Guiding Princes, just as if they were people?

NAPOLEON HILL:
Yes, or I can direct them by my thoughts. However, they need no directions, except in emergencies or under unusual circumstances, because they serve automatically, each one performing the duties assigned to him.

ALDERFER:

Do any of your princes ever let you down by failure to perform their assigned duties?

NAPOLEON HILL:

Not unless I neglect or fail to do my part in helping each of the princes to perform his duties, such, for example, as neglecting to get the proper amount of sleep, or eating the wrong combination of food. And you may be interested to know that I never fail to compensate my princes for their services. The compensation consists entirely of my daily habit of expressing gratitude for the services they render me. Each night before I go to sleep I express gratitude to each of the princes separately, thanking him for the service he has rendered me during the day, the service he will continue to render me while I sleep, and the service he will render me tomorrow.

ALDERFER:

What happens if you neglect to express your gratitude daily?

NAPOLEON HILL:

The same thing happens to the person who neglects to express gratitude daily to his Creator, and thereby removes himself from the protective powers of the Creator. I have neglected to express gratitude to my princes only a very few times, and on each occasion when I did so, the services rendered by each prince became noticeably diminished.

ALDERFER:

Through what medium and in what form do your princes communicate with you, and do they ever take the initiative in communicating?

NAPOLEON HILL:

Oh yes, they communicate freely and frequently, by the means of thoughts conveyed to me from within. They communicate with me especially when I am about to make important decisions and give me my cue as to which way I should move.

ALDERFER:

Have your princes ever given you the wrong cue?

NAPOLEON HILL:

No, as far as I know, they never have, although sometimes they inspire me to make decisions that my ordinary sense of logic rejects. In the long run, though, such decisions prove to have been the correct ones.

ALDERFER:

It would appear that you have established a relationship with your invisible friends based on the Master Mind success principle that is used by all people who rise to the upper brackets of success. Do you have other Master Mind alliances in addition to the one you have with your princes?

NAPOLEON HILL:

Oh yes, I have Master Mind alliances with other people in every field of endeavor in which I have an interest, and I have never known anyone to achieve outstanding success in any undertaking without the help of friendly allies. The Master Mind Principle is among the greatest of all the success principles because it can provide the humblest person with the wisdom and education and experience of the greatest minds.

ALDERFER:

Mr. Hill, in our last broadcast you described the three major causes of failure. Will you now give us a description of the three major causes of success?

NAPOLEON HILL:

Yes, I am happy to inform you that the three most important success principles are available to all who wish to use them. The first of these principles, of course, is Definiteness of Purpose—knowing precisely what you want and being determined to settle for nothing less than that. Here is the starting point of all successful achievement.

The second of the three most important success principles is the habit of Going the Extra Mile by rendering more service and better service than you are paid for and doing it in a pleasing mental attitude.

The third principle is the Master Mind, which consists of two or more people who blend their minds and coordinate their efforts for the attainment of a definite purpose, in a spirit of perfect harmony. These three principles are "musts" for all who wish to rise above mediocrity.

ALDERFER:
Is that your personal opinion, Mr. Hill, or is it a factual statement based upon actual experience?

NAPOLEON HILL:
It is a statement of fact based upon my observation of thousands of successful people representing almost every field of human endeavor. I never express opinions that do not have a factual foundation to justify them.

ALDERFER:
It seems to be true, from what you have just been saying, Mr. Hill, that the close association of any two or more people tends to modify the personality and the mental attitude of each person, for better or for worse. Is that your conclusion?

NAPOLEON HILL:
It's not merely my conclusion but it is a fact of such far-reaching importance that our close associates should be carefully chosen to make sure that their influence upon us is positive and not negative. For example, I have never known of a young person becoming bad or going wrong in any respect that did not begin to do so through wrong associations. Stated in another way, I have never known of a person of outstanding character who did not become

so from association with one or more persons of a similar character. And I have never known a successful business or professional man whose success did not stem from his association with some person or persons whose influence sparked his efforts with greater imagination and faith. If I had not met Andrew Carnegie, for example, I probably would still be living in the highly unfavorable environment in which I was born, instead of helping people throughout the world to better themselves.

ALDERFER:

Mr. Hill, it seems that the majority of people experience more failures than successes as they go through life. What should one do to reverse this percentage so that the successes outnumber the failures?

NAPOLEON HILL:

The first thing anyone should do following a failure or a defeat of any sort, or an unpleasant circumstance, is to begin at once to search for that seed of an equivalent benefit that comes from all such experiences. There never has been and there never will be an adversity of any sort that does not carry with it the seed of an equivalent advantage. But the usual reaction to failure and defeat is negative, and the individual stifles himself with fear and discouragement instead of taking inventory of the experience to see what advantage it may have brought.

ALDERFER:

Mr. Hill, it would be interesting, and perhaps beneficial to many of our listeners, if you gave us your idea of the type of person one should choose for close personal relationships, like marriage and intimate personal friends, and also business and professional alliances.

NAPOLEON HILL:

Without hesitation I would say that one's most helpful associates are those who inspire one to help himself. Of all the hundreds of people with whom I have been personally associated, through friendship and otherwise, the one who did more to shape my life than any other was my stepmother, who taught me early in life that self-reliance was an asset of priceless value. I am sure it was her influence that conditioned my mind not to quit when the going became hard in any sort of endeavor.

ALDERFER:

In all human relationships there are times and circumstances that cause people to become irritable and impatient with one another. What should be done when people discover that they are out of step with one another?

NAPOLEON HILL:

All successful activities are the result of harmonious relations between people. In my own relations with other people I have never permitted disharmony to prevail because I knew that if I did so, the relationship would deteriorate until it became detrimental to all concerned. Sometimes friction in human relations can be cured, but where this cannot be done, then the relationship should be dissolved. Friction in machinery and mechanical equipment is costly, but nothing in comparison with the cost of friction in human relations.

ALDERFER:

You have said, in substance, that disharmonious relations should be cured or killed? Is there no point of compromise between these two extremes?

NAPOLEON HILL:

Yes, I think there is in the relationship of marriage, where friction can be, and it should be tempered with the spirit of give and take instead of heading for the divorce courts. Marriage is the most sacred of all human relations, and it should be sanctified as such. In business and social relationships, however, friction between individuals should definitely be cured or killed, as you state it, and this for the good of all parties concerned.

ALDERFER:

In curing a relationship of disharmony and friction, where should the cure begin, of what should it consist, and who should make the first move?

NAPOLEON HILL:

The cure should begin in the hearts of all parties concerned, and it should consist of a willingness on the part of each to examine himself sincerely to make sure the seed of the discontent does not exist in his own heart. The measuring stick in this self-examination should be the Golden Rule, the greatest of all rules by which people may relate themselves to one another. Also, each individual in a controversy should remember that there are three sides to all disagreements—your side, my side, and the right side, which often is somewhere between your side and my side.

ALDERFER:

Isn't it a fact that harmony in business relations often is maintained on the basis of fear? And the same is true oftentimes in other relations as well. I have known of instances where business management maintains at the least the outward appearance of harmony by keeping employees in a state of fear.

NAPOLEON HILL:

Nothing good can come out of fear, and the business that is managed through fear sooner or later pays a high price for its mistake. The same rule applies in the management of children in the home. Love and kindness can work wonders in all human relations, but the person who endeavors to control others by fear discovers, perhaps too late, that fear comes back like a boomerang to smite the one who inspired it. Fear is the tool of the evil forces of the world. Love is the tool of the good forces and the hope of mankind. Putting it differently, you might say that fear is a weapon of the Devil, by which people are frightened into submission, while love is the medium by which the Creator bestows His benevolence.

ALDERFER:

What about people who accumulate great fortunes in business and otherwise by exploiting workers through fear? Isn't their money just as good as that which is accumulated through less cruel methods?

NAPOLEON HILL:

Anything that anyone acquires through fear, whether it be money or something else of value, has a queer way of bringing a curse on the one who accumulates it. Sometimes this curse extends to the third and even the fourth generation of the descendants of the person who brings it on himself by exploiting people through fear. If I were inclined to do so, I could give you some convincing illustrations of this truth, but most people can supply their own examples by examining the family records of men who have accumulated money by exploiting others through fear.

ALDERFER:

Mr. Hill, it strikes me rather forcefully from what you have been saying that this success philosophy has been very carefully tailored to harmonize with the natural laws of the universe.

NAPOLEON HILL:

To the best of my ability I have tested all of the success principles by the sciences and the natural laws because I learned quite early in life that all human action and all human relations that are not in harmony with the overall plan of the universe must perish through failure and defeat.

ALDERFER:

I heartily concur in what you have just said, but why is it that so many people never recognize this great universal truth?

NAPOLEON HILL:

Some very wise person once said, "Our only sin is that of ignorance." I do not pretend to know whether this is true or not, but I do know that people who do not guide their human relations in accordance with natural laws come to grief sooner or later. The Nazarene gave the world, in one short sentence, a rule for men to live by that has never been improved upon. Perhaps the simplicity of the Golden Rule invites some people to ignore its powerful potential for good in human relations.

ALDERFER:

Have you ever known of a business to be conducted strictly on the application of the Golden Rule in connection with all of its transactions?

NAPOLEON HILL:

Yes, I have known of several such businesses, and every one of them was successful, way beyond the average. Many years ago I wrote a story for a magazine based on the experience of Arthur Nash, of Cincinnati, Ohio, who resurrected his business from bankruptcy and lived to see it become one of the most profitable mail order tailoring houses in the nation. He brought about a modern business miracle by the simple procedure of adopting the Golden Rule in all of his business transactions, starting with his own employees. His success was so phenomenal, and his method of achieving it was so unique, that he received tens of thousands of dollars' worth of free publicity from magazines and newspapers throughout the country after my article appeared in which I named Mr. Nash "Golden Rule Nash."

ALDERFER:

Do you know of other cases where businesses paid off because they were operated on the Golden Rule basis?

NAPOLEON HILL:

The late Henry Ford made at least a limited application of the Golden Rule when, in 1913, he voluntarily increased the wages of all of his workers to a minimum of $5 per day when the prevailing wage was about half that amount. Those who are old enough to remember will recall that Ford's greatest financial success began with that decision. Those simple words that mean "Do unto others as if you were the others" are loaded with power sufficient to save the world from its present state of fear and frustration if only, by some miracle, we could get enough people to accept them and live by them at all levels of life.

Now may I give you my favorite epigram—Whatever Your Mind Can Conceive and Believe, Your Mind Can Achieve. Then let me sign off my giving you my favorite prayer—Oh, Divine Intelligence, I ask not for more riches, but for more wisdom with which to make better use of the blessings with which you endowed me at birth through the privilege of controlling and directing my own mind to purposes of my own choice. Amen!

ALDERFER:
Thank you, Napoleon Hill.

ANNOUNCER:
Next Sunday Napoleon Hill will be presented again over this station at the same hour. Please join us then for his discussion of the principle of Applied Faith.

△

WISDOM TO LIVE BY

Napoleon Hill states that:

1. Our brains become magnetized with the dominating thoughts that we hold in our minds, and by means with which no one is familiar, these magnets attract to us the forces, the people, and the circumstances of life that harmonize with our dominating thoughts. Luckily, we have power to control our thoughts.

2. Understanding this principle of the mind means that your economic destiny and happiness are under your total control.

3. You need assistance from no one in the manipulation of your own mind, and therefore it will function as you desire.

4. When you speak of your poverty and lack of education, you are simply directing your mind power to attract these undesirable circumstances; whatever your mind feeds upon, your mind attracts to you.

5. Your mind is something that you control, no matter what your station in life may be, provided always that you exercise the right instead of permitting others to do so for you.

ADVERSITY AND ADVANTAGE

Napoleon Hill talks about three types of defeat:

1. The loss of material things, such as wealth, position, and property.

2. Loss resulting from opposition growing out of friction in human relationships or differing belief systems.

3. Defeat from within, wherein you lose contact with the spiritual forces of being.

The first two are easy to recover from, by looking for the seed of equal or greater benefit. However, when you experience the third type of defeat, you really feel it deeply. It happens only when you are not in harmony with Nature's laws. Make sure that all your actions and human relations are in harmony with the overall plan of the universe. Once you learn this, there never will be an adversity you cannot handle.

▼

CHAPTER 6

HOW TO DEVELOP THE POWER OF APPLIED FAITH

(THE POWER BEYOND SCIENCE)

"Affliction comes to us all, not to make us sad, but sober; not to make us sorry, but to make us wise; not to make us despondent, but by its darkness to refresh us as the night refreshes the day; not to impoverish, but to enrich us."

Henry Ward Beecher

OVERVIEW

The purpose of this chapter is to introduce you to your Other Self, the self that has a vision of your innate spiritual power and that will not accept or recognize failure.

Napoleon Hill makes you aware of this unbounded power that:

• Can open the doors to your success

• Can guide you toward your goal without much effort on your part

• When combined with purpose and a positive mental attitude, can make you limitless

• Will eliminate hardships and misery from your life

• Will condition you to consciously and, with practice, unconsciously tap into the power of Infinite Intelligence

Napoleon Hill's step-by-step process described in this chapter will help you to develop this amazing power to make the impossible possible in your life.

BROADCAST 6. HOW TO DEVELOP THE POWER OF APPLIED FAITH

ANNOUNCER:

Success Unlimited is on the air, presenting once more the distinguished success philosopher Napoleon Hill, whose success books are now published and distributed as bestsellers in every civilized country, where they have benefitted millions of people. Today Napoleon Hill brings you an idea that, if you are ready to accept it, can change not only your own life for the better, but it can change as well your entire community or the place where you are occupied in your work, as well as the mental atmosphere of your own home. And now here is Henry Alderfer, associate director of education of the Napoleon Hill Institute, who will assist Napoleon Hill on this program. Mr. Alderfer.

ALDERFER:

Thank you. Our radio audience has a treat in store this afternoon because Napoleon Hill will present his interpretation of the power of Applied Faith—one that will open doors to success that previously have been closed and seemingly locked. Listen carefully because the message Napoleon Hill brings you today has helped millions of people throughout the world to give their lives a new meaning.

NAPOLEON HILL:

Good afternoon, my radio friends, may I come in for a visit which might well be the beginning of a personal friendship that will enrich the lives of both you and me? During my visit this afternoon I wish to talk to you about the most important person now living, as far as you are concerned, and that person is yourself. More than four decades ago I sat in the private library of the then richest man in the world and heard him make a prediction that seemed to promise me the impossible. That man was Andrew Carnegie, founder of the great United States Steel Corporation, who had just commissioned me to organize the world's first practical philosophy of success. "If you carry out the mission I have assigned you," said Mr. Carnegie, "you will live to see the day when you will be richer than I am, and you will have made more successful people than I have been responsible for, provided that you discover the power of faith and learn to be guided by it."

ALDERFER:

That was quite a promise to make to an unknown youth such as you were at that time, wasn't it?

NAPOLEON HILL:

Yes, it was! But it was no more startling than the promise I shall now make to every listener to this program this afternoon, namely, if you are ready and you will follow the instructions I shall give you, your future will yield you everything you have hoped for in the past but did not get, or a reasonable equivalent thereof.

ALDERFER:
Before you give the instructions, will you tell our audience how Mr. Carnegie's prediction concerning you turned out?

NAPOLEON HILL:
Henry, there are several million men and women throughout the world who could answer your question more modestly than I can answer it, because they have received great benefits as the result of their introduction by me to Andrew Carnegie's formula for Applied Faith. But to be more specific, I would say that Mr. Carnegie's prophesy was a gross understatement of what was to happen, because I have already been responsible for vastly more successes than were inspired by Mr. Carnegie, and as far as riches are concerned, my greatest asset is one I wish to share with the listeners on our program with the hope that it will bring them abundance in those of life's values that count for the most.

ALDERFER:
I know you have a very practical formula for the development and application of Applied Faith. Will you describe it to our radio audience?

NAPOLEON HILL:
The very foundation of Applied Faith is a burning desire for the attainment of definite objectives, plans, or purposes. When Andrew Carnegie predicted that I would become richer than he and make more successful people than he had made, his words would have been meaningless if I had not believed what he said.

ALDERFER:
But at the time that Mr. Carnegie made that prophecy you were a young, unknown man with but little, if anything, to justify your believing that you

could surpass the great Carnegie. Just how did you go about conditioning your mind to believe that which seemed impossible?

NAPOLEON HILL:
To be frank I didn't believe it at first, but Mr. Carnegie gave me a formula that lifted me to a higher plane of understanding, and it was through that formula that I discovered my Other Self—the self that knows no such thing as the impossible.

ALDERFER:
Now you're becoming interesting, indeed. Will you reveal the nature of the formula and describe how it worked for you?

NAPOLEON HILL:
Like all truly great things, the formula was surprisingly simple. Mr. Carnegie explained to me that everyone is a dual personality, with one self—the one we know best, unfortunately—being a negative personality who is the victim of self-imposed limitations, and the Other Self—the one we do not recognize—being a personality who recognizes that whatever the mind can conceive and believe the mind can achieve.

ALDERFER:
How did you discover your Other Self, and by what means did you induce it to take over and help you fulfill Mr. Carnegie's prediction?

NAPOLEON HILL:
You are going to be surprised when I tell you, and you will perhaps be even more surprised if you adopt the formula that Mr. Carnegie gave me and carry it out as faithfully as I did. He instructed me to devote two short periods daily to talking to myself in front of a mirror, one upon arising in the morning, the other before retiring at night.

ALDERFER:
What did he tell you to say to yourself?

NAPOLEON HILL:
He gave me a speech to follow, and I followed it to the letter. The speech was this: "Your Creator gave you exclusive power of control over your thoughts, and He gave you the privilege of believing you can achieve any purpose you set your heart upon. I believe I shall excel Andrew Carnegie in the making of successful people, and I see this as an accomplished end."

ALDERFER:
Was this all there was to the speech?

NAPOLEON HILL:
Yes, that was all, and it was enough! If you will study the wording of that short speech carefully, you may discover that it contains the sum and the substance of the power behind all great achievements. That word "believe" is the central core of the entire speech. It led me to the discovery of my Other Self—and it led me to the discovery that my only limitations were those that I set up for myself through the neglect of belief.

ALDERFER:
But, isn't it true that one must have some reasonable foundation upon which to establish belief? Doesn't one have to reason using facts and logic, as well as past experiences?

NAPOLEON HILL:
Let me answer you this way—when facts, past experiences, and logic serve to help you attain that which you seek, they should be relied upon, but if these fall short of attainment of your objectives, you have the privilege of circumventing these orthodox guideposts and hitching yourself to the star of faith—that mysterious power which can perform miracles.

Belief operates through the power of the subconscious mind, and it is an established fact that the subconscious will accept and carry out to its logical conclusion any instruction given to it in that state of mind known as faith.

ALDERFER:

Oh, I see what you mean! Tell your subconscious mind what you desire often enough, and it will guide you to its attainment by perfectly natural means. Is that the idea?

NAPOLEON HILL:

Well, not quite. You omitted one important item, namely, that your state of mind while you are giving the instructions is the determining factor as to what happens afterward. You see, your subconscious mind is a silent listener to all of your words and to all of your thoughts. When I first began delivering that speech in front of a mirror I did not entirely believe what I was saying. But by repetition of the speech I soon began to believe what I was saying, and then things began to happen in my favor.

ALDERFER:

What keeps one's belief alive when logic, facts, and past experiences do not support it?

NAPOLEON HILL:

Brace yourself for a shock, because I've just been waiting for that question. The thing that keeps one's belief alive when there is no apparent justification for it is a burning desire for the attainment of definite objectives. You can desire anything. Your Creator has generously provided that you are the sole master over your desires. He has also provided you with a miraculous power by which you may translate your desires into their physical equivalent. It consists in the law of Cosmic Habitforce, through which your habits, both of acts and of thoughts, are picked up and carried out to their logical conclusion.

ALDERFER:

How wonderful! And right here we are rubbing elbows with the supreme secret of all great successes, because it is an established fact that all thoughts tend to clothe themselves in their physical equivalents—the things to which they are akin.

NAPOLEON HILL:

Yes, that is correct, and you can begin now to see the purpose behind Mr. Carnegie's request that I speak to myself in front of a mirror, and, you may be interested in knowing that it was this experience which led me finally to the discovery of my silent partners known as the Nine Guiding Princes.

ALDERFER:

Has it been your observation that all achievements in the upper brackets of success have been sparked by the power of enduring faith?

NAPOLEON HILL:

Yes, great achievements in all walks of life begin first in the form of Definiteness of Purpose, backed by a burning desire for its attainment, and this is refined into belief in the attainment. Thomas Edison believed he could perfect an incandescent electric lamp, and that belief carried him to final victory after more than ten thousand failures. Marconi believed the ether could be made to carry the vibrations of sound without the use of wires, and he carried on through many failures until he was rewarded by triumph. Helen Keller believed she would learn to communicate despite the fact she had lost her power of sight and hearing, and her belief brought her inevitable victory. Henry Ford believed he could build a horseless buggy that would provide rapid transportation within the financial means of all, and despite the far-flung cry of skepticism he encountered, he belted the earth with his product and made himself fabulously rich in the bargain.

ALDERFER:

Aren't there some other success principles that can be used to give one access to Applied Faith more rapidly?

NAPOLEON HILL:

Yes, there are three other success principles that are closely related to Faith. These are Definiteness of Purpose, the Master Mind, and Going the Extra Mile. Combine these with Applied Faith, and you have what is called the Big Four success principles that are largely responsible for all great successes.

ALDERFER:

To sum up what you have been saying, the proper procedure in developing the power of Applied Faith is this: Determine definitely what you desire, then fan this into a white heat of burning desire by giving your subconscious mind daily instructions to guide you to the object of your desire. Follow this procedure until you succeed, even though logic, fact, and past experiences may not necessarily support you.

NAPOLEON HILL:

Yes, that about tells the story, but let us not overlook the fact that when we receive guidance through the subconscious mind, we must do our part by earning the right to that which we seek. There is no such reality as something for nothing, and Nature has no bargain basement counters, as Emerson so well pointed out in his essay *Compensation*.

ALDERFER:

Why is it necessary to repeat one's desire when seeking the aid of the subconscious mind?

NAPOLEON HILL:

Repetition of a thought, plan, or purpose, by bringing it into the mind often and expressing it orally, serves to clearly outline the mental picture of that which one desires, so the subconscious mind may act upon the desire intelligently. The subconscious mind will not act on any idea plan or purpose that is not clearly presented to it. Study that statement carefully, and it may provide the key to a clear understanding of the potential powers of faith. Faith is guidance! It is nothing more. It will not bring you that which you seek, but it will show you the path by which you may go after it.

Faith is a state of mind—a positive mental attitude. And mental attitude is the only thing over which an individual has absolute power of control and direction. Exercise of this privilege carries with it stupendous benefits. Neglect to exercise it brings terrific penalties. Faith, expressed through a positive mental attitude, built the world's greatest single-span suspension bridge, the Golden Gate Bridge in San Francisco, after its builder, chief engineer Joseph Strauss, had been refused the necessary funds with which to proceed when the first abutments tumbled into the sea before the wires had been strung. Faith is hopes, wishes, and beliefs condensed into a positive state of mind that defies analysis and helps people to do the impossible.

Faith made Harry S Truman president of the United States, in 1948, when practically everyone, including his own influential party leaders, believed his election to be impossible. And faith helped Franklin D. Roosevelt turn back the tides of the worst state of fear this nation has ever known, and that same power kept him in office until his death.

ALDERFER:
Were not the experiences of Captain Eddie Rickenbacker, including his crash in the ocean during World War II, when he and members of his crew survived for twenty-four days without food, a miraculous illustration of the power of faith?

NAPOLEON HILL:
Nothing could have saved Rickenbacker and his crew except his unyielding faith. And it was that same unshakable faith that has enabled Eddie Rickenbacker to take over the practically bankrupt Eastern Airlines and develop it into one of the great transportation systems of our nation. Nothing is impossible to the person who has the sort of faith that kept Captain

Rickenbacker alive out there in the cold waters of the ocean for twenty-four days, when all reason and all logic plainly said he couldn't survive. And the remarkable part of Rickenbacker's experience is the fact that he established a Master Mind relationship with his crew by which he transmuted his faith to them so they could survive. Somehow men of great faith have a way of inspiring those around them to do the seemingly impossible.

ALDERFER:

In view of the comparative simplicity with which one may develop and use the power of faith, why is it that the vast majority of people never avail themselves of this miraculous power?

NAPOLEON HILL:

That's a very good question, and I think I can give you the correct answer. Most people keep their minds fixed on the things and circumstances they do not desire and naturally these are what they attract. The successful people in all walks of life keep their minds fixed on the things they desire, and the same law that brings failure to others brings them success on their own terms.

ALDERFER:

We come now to the big question that undoubtedly is on everyone's mind— what gives such miraculous powers to the state of mind known as faith? What is the source of power that can be contacted and drawn upon by the application of faith?

NAPOLEON HILL:

You have asked the sixty-four-dollar question, sure enough, but the answer is obvious. The source that one may draw upon through faith is the same power that operates the world we live in and the universe of which we are an infinitesimal part. And man is the only living creature who has been provided with the means of tapping this power and directing it to ends of his own choice.

ALDERFER:

Your explanation seems so very simple, yet it explains the most profound of all truths. And it provides, for those who are ready for it, a formula by which they may write their own price tag and establish their own way of living, including the accumulation of all the material riches they desire. Have I stated the potentials of the power of faith too strongly?

NAPOLEON HILL:

Henry, there are no words in the English language with which one could exaggerate the possibilities of human achievement through the power of faith. For example, let us turn back the pages of the book of time and briefly review what has been accomplished during the first half of this century through the application of faith. We have seen Andrew Carnegie, a poor emigrant lad from Scotland, usher in the great steel age that made possible hundreds of kindred industries and gave employment to millions of people. We have seen Thomas Edison bring in, through his power of faith, the great electrical age that lightens man's labors in thousands of ways and provides employment for huge armies of men and women. We have seen Henry Ford put the whole world on wheels through the product of his imagination and the power of his faith. Mr. Marconi has shown us how to harness the ether and make it give us a means of communication without the aid of wires. Lee DeForest has given us radio and television. We have seen Luther Burbank strip the thorns from the cactus and interbreed flowers into color combinations that far excel the previous work of Nature. We have seen the Wright Brothers conquer the air and pave the way for travel by air coaches at a speed of three hundred miles per hour and more. We have seen the development of radar that gives us the power with which to detect objects beyond the reach of the human eye. We have seen learned doctors stop the ravages of typhoid fever, yellow fever, smallpox, and myriad other diseases that plagued the human race until but recent years. We have seen engineers build skyscraper buildings reaching upward for fifty stories and more. And the most profound part of this story of man's achievements through Applied Faith consists in the fact that the men who were responsible for these blessings were just ordinary, everyday types of people, many of them, such as Thomas Edison, Henry Ford. and Andrew Carnegie, having had little formal education.

ALDERFER:

What you have just been saying is that no one has a monopoly on the power of faith, and the humblest person may appropriate this power for the attainment of purposes of his own choice. Despite this fact, aren't there many people who hesitate to undertake the creation of new ideas because they believe everything that is worthwhile has already been revealed?

NAPOLEON HILL:

Yes, there are people like that, and they are the very people we are seeking to inspire through these radio programs.

ALDERFER:

Isn't it true, Mr. Hill, that a Master Mind alliance provides the best of all means of developing and applying the power of faith?

NAPOLEON HILL:

Yes, the great achievements of the past fifty years have been the results of combinations of minds working together in a spirit of harmony. And I sincerely regret that I could not include in my list of some of the great achievements of the past fifty years, the existence of a practical system through which men and women could pool their physical, mental, and spiritual powers in some form of labor of love that would make this a better world in which to live. It's a gross understatement of the truth when I say that the combined faith of one hundred people, or less, applied under the Master Mind Principle, could change our entire American way of life so as to eliminate the sinful waste caused by friction in human relations.

ALDERFER:

Perhaps this broadcast will give someone an idea that can be developed into the Master Mind alliance you have just mentioned.

NAPOLEON HILL:

I mentioned the possibilities of such an alliance for that very purpose, and I would suggest that the first objective of the alliance should be that of eliminating the cold war that is being waged between management and organized labor. I am hoping that I shall see the day when I may join forces with an able labor leader who will allow me to help him run his union on the basis of the Golden Rule. And I am hoping, also, that I shall live to see the day when I may donate my services to some industrialist or business owner who will permit me to lend him my faith in a system of employer-employee relations that will make strikes impossible because there will be no cause for strikes.

ALDERFER:

You spoke of the cold war now being waged between management and organized labor. Isn't it true that the war is a hot war at times?

NAPOLEON HILL:

Yes, that is correct! And it is a form of human behavior unworthy of a great country like ours, where human freedom is our greatest boast, and individual opportunities surpass those available anywhere in the world.

ALDERFER:

Mr. Hill, it seems to me that you have put yourself out on a limb by publicly offering to donate your services to both organized labor and industrial management. Are you really serious about this?

NAPOLEON HILL:

I was never more serious in my life. Moreover, my offer extends not only to both management and labor, but also to individuals as well! You see, my entire life has been devoted to helping people to unlock and use the great powers that are available to them through Applied Faith. I have now passed the midday of life and have reached the afternoon. From here on out I wish to multiply myself by a few thousands of sincere men and women who will enter into Master Mind alliances with me in order that we may help each of these people to find a better way of life and at the same time give the world a healthy demonstration of the powers of the Golden Rule in all human relations.

ALDERFER:
Your idea seems marvelous. Has any such a plan been tried out that you know about?

NAPOLEON HILL:
Yes, I know of at least a dozen businesses that operate successfully on the Golden Rule basis, where the employees receive better wages than the average and the businesses earn greater profits than the average. But the most encouraging demonstration I have seen took place in the little town of Paris, Missouri, a few years ago, when ninety-three men and women formed a Master Mind alliance and began cooperating with one another on the Golden Rule basis after they had attended a series of my lectures on the success principles I had organized. They organized themselves under the name of Club Success Unlimited, and they have literally performed miracles that have benefitted not only themselves but that entire community.

ALDERFER:
I have heard of the Paris, Missouri, experiment. In fact, I have met some of the members of the group that inaugurated the Paris plan. Will you describe what these people have accomplished under the plan?

NAPOLEON HILL:
Time will permit only a brief description of a portion of the results, but you can get a fair idea of what happened from the remarks of a citizen of Paris, who was not even a member of the group, when he said, "I have lived here for seventy years, and in all that time I have never seen anything or any influence that has so improved the relations of our people as has this success club group."

ALDERFER:

Will you give us some individual cases of what happened to those who belonged to the group in Paris?

NAPOLEON HILL:

Well, there was Dr. Barnett, a local physician whose office was located in a one-room, run-down frame building. He caught the spirit of friendly coordination of effort through his alliance with the others and built one of the finest medical clinics to be found in Missouri. The building is on a main business street, and it inspired other business and professional men to follow suit by improving their properties.

A lady member of the group was associated with the local public school as a teacher, at ordinary teacher's wages. Her association with the success group inspired her to start a business in ceramics during her spare time, which pays her more than her job as a teacher.

A local clergyman, Dr. Bailey, headed a Protestant church with a stated membership of some four hundred, not more than thirty-five of whom regularly attended his Sunday services. Through his association with the success group he filled his church to overflowing. Moreover, the non-attending members not only became attending members, but they became paying members as well, for they donated the money to give the church building an entire face-lifting.

ALDERFER:

And all of this happened within a matter of a few years?

NAPOLEON HILL:

Yes, but wait! You haven't heard the half of it yet. A young man member of the group worked in a gasoline filling station. As the result of the faith he acquired from his alliance with the others, he went into business for himself, and he now owns and operates four large freight and express moving vans. Doc Gutherie, a local plumber, was a member of the success group. His shop was in a small basement out of sight, where it was hard to find. Through his association with the group, he acquired the faith that enabled him to build one of the finest showrooms on Main Street in Paris, and it is stocked with a wide range of electrical appliances of every description, and his business has doubled many times. The Mark Twain Café, which employed Carl Bodits, a young chef from Chicago, was about to close up because of a lack of business when he joined the success group. Through the faith he acquired by association with the group, he now owns the café. He has built himself a fine new home, bought a new car, and has a business that he could sell for a handsome figure. A carpenter who joined the success group gained enough faith from his association with the group to promote himself into a very fine position as a salesman in which he earns many times what he made from carpentering.

ALDERFER:
Isn't that wonderful. It sounds almost like *Alice in Wonderland*.

NAPOLEON HILL:
Yes, it is wonderful indeed, and it gives you a fair idea of what can happen when every village, town, and city in America learns about the Paris story and begins to emulate it. Then the people of any town could so change their human relations that everyone would be happy and prosperous.

ALDERFER:
Some great power for good must have come into the lives of the people of Paris. Could you identify this power?

NAPOLEON HILL:
Very easily! They were simply following the principle of Applied Faith! Previously they had been merely talking about faith and professing to believe in it but doing nothing to make it work in their daily lives.

ALDERFER:
Do you believe the people in other small towns, like Paris, Missouri, are as ready for a better way of living as were the members of the Paris success group?

NAPOLEON HILL:

People are people, no matter where they live, and their problems, their needs, their motives are pretty much the same. Yes, there is a golden opportunity to duplicate the Paris story in every small town and village in America, indeed, in the world!

ANNOUNCER:

You have just heard Napoleon Hill. This was another program in the Success School of the Air—Success Unlimited. Next Sunday at the same hour Napoleon Hill will be presented over this station. His subject will be How to Develop a Winning Personality. Don't miss it because it may give you a better look at yourself.

△

WISDOM TO LIVE BY

1. Your mind has been provided with a gateway to approach the Infinite Intelligence through what is known as the subconscious mind.

2. Napoleon Hill talks about the power of faith, which means having confidence, trust, and an absolute belief that you can do something. This power of faith comes to us from a Higher Source.

3. Faith is a state of mind that results in conditioning your mind to establish a working association with the Universal Power. Applied Faith is the adaptation of the power received to fulfilling our goals.

4. We all have been equipped by the Creator with certain faculties that enable us to enter into a definite, positive relationship with this Infinite Power and to apply it to fulfilling our goals.

5. Napoleon Hill gives three easy steps to create a state of mind known as faith.

   a. Express a burning desire for the achievement of your definite major purpose and relate it to one or more of the basic motives.

b. Create a definite and specific plan for the attainment of your burning desire.

c. Start acting upon your plan immediately, putting every conscious effort behind it.

ADVERSITY AND ADVANTAGE

1. Once you have made up your mind to do something definite, adversities will still come along to prevent you from being successful if they can. These are simply to test your faith. The more testing your faith endures, the stronger it will become.

2. When such temporary defeats come, accept them as inspiration for greater effort and determination on your part. Carry on with the belief that you will succeed. Be sure that you are rendering service equal to or better in value than the riches you are seeking. Faith will give you the power to convert adversities and temporary defeats into an equal force for good.

▼

CHAPTER 7

HOW TO DEVELOP A WINNING PERSONALITY

(PREREQUISITE TO BECOME A GREAT LEADER)

△

"Let me embrace thee, sour adversity, for wise
men say it is the wisest course."

Shakespeare

OVERVIEW

In this chapter you will learn one of the most valuable skills necessary for success: the ability to influence others without annoying them.

Hill will reveal why a winning personality is so important to success and what you must do to achieve it. You will learn the answers to these critical questions:

- Why is it important to have a harmonious relationship with others?

- What is the essential asset for the accumulation of all riches?

- What trait do I need in order to convert defeat into victory?

- How do I attract the friendly cooperation of others?

Understanding these concepts will allow you to acquire the essential skills for influencing others. With this knowledge, you can transform yourself into a magnetic person to attract the right people to cooperate with you for your success.

BROADCAST 7. HOW TO DEVELOP A WINNING PERSONALITY

ANNOUNCER:

Success Unlimited is on the air, presenting once more the distinguished success philosopher Napoleon Hill, whose success books are now published and distributed as bestsellers in every civilized country, where they have benefitted millions of people. Today Napoleon Hill brings you an idea and makes you a promise that, if you are ready to accept it, can change not only your own life for the better, but it can change as well your entire community or the place where you are occupied in your work, as well as the mental atmosphere of your own home. And now here is Henry Alderfer, associate director of education of the Napoleon Hill Institute, who will assist Napoleon Hill on this program. Mr. Alderfer.

ALDERFER:

Thank you. This afternoon we are going to give you a very important principle in the philosophy of success, namely, that of How to Develop a Winning Personality. Our personality is the sum total of everything that constitutes our individual mental, emotional, and temperamental makeup. I understand, Mr. Hill, that you have separated the factors of personality into specific traits, and you have identified thirty factors of a pleasing personality. However, time doesn't permit us to cover all of these, but we will discuss a few of the more important ones.

Now here is Napoleon Hill, who has spent most of his life proving the soundness of the principle he is going to talk about this afternoon.

NAPOLEON HILL:

Good afternoon, my radio friends. We will begin with the most important of these traits of a pleasing personality, which is a positive mental attitude. You can get a good idea of the important part a positive mental attitude plays in your life by considering the fact that it influences your tone of voice, the expression on your face, and the posture of your body, and it modifies every word that you speak, as well as determining the nature of your emotions. Actually, it does more than these. It affects every thought you release, thereby extending your influence to all who come within your range.

Just for the sake of illustration, let us list some of the disagreeable things that a bad mental attitude causes. They are as follows: it dampens your enthusiasm, curtails your initiative, overthrows your self-control, subdues your imagination, undermines your desire to be cooperative, makes you sullen and intolerant, and throws your reasoning power out of gear.

ALDERFER:

How would a negative mental attitude affect a professional person, for instance, a lawyer or a teacher or a doctor?

NAPOLEON HILL:

A lawyer who goes into court with a bad or negative mental attitude may find the judge and jury opposing him, although he may have a perfectly just case. The teacher who goes into his classroom with the same kind of attitude will get that same negative reaction from his students, and the doctor who comes into the presence of his patients with a negative mental attitude may do more harm than good. A man may have all the culture modern civilization can provide; he may have a number of degrees after his name; he may be the most skilled man in his field, but he will be a failure if he carries a bad mental attitude around with him. The one thing that people will not tolerate is a negative mental attitude.

ALDERFER:

I understand that Mr. Carnegie's right-hand man, Charles Schwab, was paid a great deal, both as a salary and a bonus. What was the real power behind Mr. Schwab?

NAPOLEON HILL:

When you analyze Mr. Schwab's personality in minute detail, you will find why he became the successful man that he was. Schwab came to Carnegie as an ordinary laborer. He had but little schooling and very few special talents in anything, but he did have one important asset that will give you the clue to his success. He had a perfect mental attitude toward himself and all others with whom he came in contact.

ALDERFER:

Where and how did he come by that attitude?

NAPOLEON HILL:

He probably was born with a flexible background for the cultivation of such an attitude, but he acquired the habit of expanding it because he was associated with a group of men who made it a part of their daily duty to develop and maintain a positive mental attitude.

Before we pass on to another factor of a pleasing personality, let me say that this subject of a positive mental attitude will show up for consideration in every one of the other qualities of personality we will analyze. It is definitely related to all of them, a fact that is very significant.

The salesman who begins his day with a negative mental attitude may take some old orders, but he will sell nothing, and he would be better off if he remained at home until his mental attitude improved. He will not only make no sales when he is in a negative mental attitude, but he will very probably make enemies and lose customers.

The ballplayer who goes into the pitcher's box with a negative mental attitude will be practically sure to lose control over the ball, to say nothing of incurring the ill will of the fans in the grandstand.

The motorist with a negative mental attitude becomes a menace to other motorists, although he may be an expert at the wheel. Traffic officials report that a major portion of all automobile accidents are caused by motorists who are irritable and are, therefore, negligent in their driving habits.

ALDERFER:

I am beginning to understand why these factors are so important, because everything we do and every contact we have with others is a measure of our personality. There is another trait that I think is very important, and this is the trait that we will call flexibility. What do we mean by flexibility?

NAPOLEON HILL:

Flexibility consists of the habit of adapting oneself to quickly changing circumstances without losing one's sense of composure. A man with a flexible disposition must be something of a chameleon, able to quickly change color to harmonize with the environment. Andrew Carnegie said that flexibility was one quality that made Charles Schwab one of America's greatest salesmen. He could get down on the ground and play a game of marbles with a group of boys, then get up and walk into his office and be ready to enter a Master Mind meeting where he was called upon to make decisions involving millions of dollars.

A person who lacks the quality of flexibility will not be a good leader in business or industry or in any kind of supervisory position where success depends upon the cooperation of others. The foreman in a factory who has flexibility of personality may have the fullest cooperation of all of his men because he will relate himself to each man according to that man's personality.

Life is one continuous series of experiences in salesmanship through which one must sell himself to every person he meets in his social, professional, or occupational contacts, and if one lacks a pleasing personality to enable him to harmonize his mental attitude with the people with whom he comes in contact, he will not be a successful salesman of himself.

ALDERFER:

I have heard that another very important trait is promptness of decision, and successful men are successful because they reach decisions definitely and quickly and become annoyed by others who didn't act promptly. What is your reaction to that statement?

NAPOLEON HILL:

When you observe people, you will notice that those who dillydally trying to make up their minds but never seem to get around to it, are never popular or successful. This is a fast-moving world of action, and those who don't move quickly and definitely only get in the way of those who know where they are going and what they are seeking.

Promptness of decision is related to definiteness of purpose, the starting point of all individual achievement that is worthy of note, and we're living in a world where individual achievement is possible on a grand scale because of the great abundance of opportunities in every calling. But opportunity waits for no man. The man with vision to recognize opportunity and the promptness of decision to embrace it will get ahead. The others will be the followers, and will lag far, far behind.

ALDERFER:

It is very interesting to note that every person who develops a winning personality must study his own face and place it under his control so he can make it convey any feeling he desires. In other words, he must use his face, and he must have a pleasing tone of voice; he must put life into that voice with the habit of smiling, and the dramatization of the voice can be illustrated by the expression on his face. These three characteristics—the tone of the voice, the habit of smiling, and facial expression—tell a great deal about a person, don't they?

NAPOLEON HILL:
Yes, they do. The spoken word is the medium by which one expresses his personality most effectively. The tone of the voice, therefore, should be so definitely under control that it can be colored and modified so as to make it convey any desired meaning quite in addition to the words used. The successful salesman, clergyman, teacher, lawyer, and professional speaker who makes his living by talking habitually controls the tone of his voice. By this means, words are dramatized and given a desired meaning. A man with a winning personality knows how to convey his emotions and does so by the modification of the tone of his voice. He can express anger, fear, curiosity, contempt, danger, grudge, sincerity, derision, anxiety, and a wide range of other emotions by the control of the tone of his voice. The price of perfection in this trait, as it is in so many others, is eternal practice and patience.

ALDERFER:
I understand that the habit of smiling is also a very valuable trait to use in order to get along with people.

NAPOLEON HILL:
Yes, it is, and this habit, like many others, is directly related to the individual's mental attitude, and it discloses the nature of his mental attitude with almost perfect means of identification. If you are not concerned about the relationship between the habit of smiling and the mental attitude, just try smiling when you are angry and notice how quickly you will change from a negative to a positive state. The most successful people in practically every

calling are those who understand the art of dramatization of their speech. They can tell a story, request a favor, give an order, or even reprimand an associate in such a manner that their words have a telling and lasting effect, and they can do it with a smile on their face.

ALDERFER:

I understand, then, that the traits of personality can be enhanced by anyone who desires to make himself pleasing, and considering the fact that one's personality is his greatest asset or his greatest liability, there can be no legitimate excuse for failure to improve it. This brings us to the third of these traits, namely, facial expression. I have heard it said that a competent character analyst can tell by a glance at the expression on one's face, the nature of his character. Is this true? Are character analysts the only people who can do this, or does everyone do it, consciously or unconsciously?

NAPOLEON HILL:

You can learn a great deal of what is going on in a person's mind by the expression on his face, just as you may judge what a dog may be thinking about by the expression on its face and the wag of its tail. Dogs too can smile, and they do when they are friendly, and they do it by the expression on their faces and with a wag of their tail. A smile produces one arrangement of the line of facial muscles, while a frown produces an entirely different arrangement, but each of them conveys with unerring accuracy the feeling that is taking place in the mind of a person.

Lawyers who are clever at questioning witnesses in court often have a great ability to judge by the expression on a witness's face when the witness is lying and when he is telling the truth. Master salesmen follow the same rule. They can detect by careful observation of their prospective purchaser's face what the nature of his thoughts are. Thus, the smile, the tone of voice, and the expression on the face constitute open windows through which all who will may see and feel what takes place in the minds of people. A smart person will know when to keep these windows closed. He will also know when to open them.

For the purpose of remembering these three openings to the mind, we might call them the "Big Three" traits of a winning personality, namely, the smile, facial expression, and the tone of voice.

ALDERFER:

That's very interesting, and I can understand now why we have some people who are called "poker faces" and also some who can't hide anything, because these "Big Three" give away their inner most thoughts.

There is another trait that fits right in with these, which says that there is always a right time and a wrong time for anything. I think our listeners know that we mean tactfulness. We know that this trait has its place in our dealings with people. What is the part that tactfulness plays in our association with others?

NAPOLEON HILL:

Tactfulness consists in doing and saying the right thing at the right time, and here are some of the ways in which people show their lack of tactfulness: The habit of speaking out of turn, interrupting the speech of others, asking impertinent questions, going where one is not invited, holding people on the telephone with useless conversation, challenging the soundness of the opinions of others, speaking disparagingly of others, correcting subordinates and associates in the presence of others, complaining when requests for favors are received, using profane language, expressing one's dislike too freely, and the habit of trying to minimize another person's achievements.

ALDERFER:

These are very interesting, and most of us have one or more of these traits that hinder us from having a winning personality. If we would check our personality by this list just mentioned, we could make great discoveries of benefit to ourselves.

I understand another important trait of a winning personality is tolerance. Someone once stated that intolerance has held back the advancement of civilization a thousand years. This might be an understatement, but what is the real meaning of tolerance?

NAPOLEON HILL:
Tolerance consists of an open mind on all subjects toward all people and at all times. An intolerant person has fixed opinions on almost every subject, and he generally expresses his opinions freely and will not listen to the opinions of others. He makes his own rules of personal conduct to accommodate his personal whims, likes, and dislikes. Such a person is usually unpopular. The intolerant person never seems to learn the truth about the effects of expressing his opinions but continues to be an offender, which leads one to wonder whether intolerance is really a negative trait of personality or an incurable disease.

ALDERFER:
That seems to be an interesting observation because I know that intolerance limits an individual's privilege of appropriating and using the knowledge and experience of others. You have found in your research that it does certain other things as well. Would you name a few?

NAPOLEON HILL:
I'll be glad to. It makes enemies of those who would otherwise be friends; it stops the growth of the mind by eliminating the search for knowledge; and it prohibits self-discipline and accuracy in thinking and reasoning.

ALDERFER:
A great philosopher expressed his views on this subject of intolerance in a personal creed he wrote to guard himself against this evil. Will you give this to our radio audience?

NAPOLEON HILL:
"Let me be open-minded on all subjects so that I may grow mentally and spiritually. May the time never come when I will be above learning from

the humblest person. Let me never forget that a closed mind is a narrow mind. May I never fall into the habit of expressing opinions on any subject unless they are founded upon reasonably dependable knowledge. Forbid that I should ever find fault with anyone because he may not agree with my opinions on any subject. Restrain me, always, Oh Power of Reason, from speaking out of turn where I have not been invited to speak. May I always show a wholesome respect for those with whom I may not agree. Keep me ever reminded that the thing I know best is that I know too little about anything, that the sum total of knowledge acquired by the whole of mankind is not enough to justify any man in boasting of his knowledge. Give me the courage to admit that I do not know the answer when I am asked a question regarding anything about which I know but little or nothing. May I always share willingly with others such humble knowledge as I may possess that could be of help to others. And never let me forget that humility of the heart will attract more friends than will all the wisdom of mankind. Let me remain always a student in search of truth, and may I never pretend to be a finished scholar on any subject. May I always remember that the greatest of all privileges is that of expressing tolerance by example. And never let me forget the words 'Hope, Faith, and Charity.'"

ALDERFER:
There is another important trait of personality without which a person can't seem to get along in life, especially in these tense days.

NAPOLEON HILL:
Oh yes, I know what you mean, and that's a keen sense of humor. Anyone without it leaves others under the impression that he has an exaggerated feeling of superiority and labors under the apprehension that his dominating manner must be respected. A well-developed sense of humor aids one in becoming flexible and adjustable to varying circumstances of life. It also enables him to relax and become human instead of appearing cool and distant, a trait that doesn't attract friends. This is the day and age when

a sense of humor keeps one from taking himself and life too seriously, a tendency toward which many people are inclined.

The person who cannot relax and laugh at the proper time is to be pitied, for he will miss the better portion of life's benefits, no matter what his other assets may be. He needs some method of escape from his routine occupation, and this sense of humor enables him to break the hold of monotony. A smile drives away many a worry and a frown. A sense of humor also protects one against becoming intolerant, and evidence of this is found in the fact that practically all intolerant people wear a sober expression on their faces, as if the weight of the world rested on their shoulders.

ALDERFER:
Wouldn't it be wonderful if we had all the time we needed to discuss all of these qualities of a winning personality, because from what you have been saying, it seems very difficult to pick out some of the qualities and eliminate others.

NAPOLEON HILL:
Yes, it is, Henry, and it might be appropriate that we spend a short time on a few of the remaining ones to give our listeners an idea about them. For example, we know that we cannot become popular unless we get along with others and are just. A keen sense of justice is a very important trait.

ALDERFER:
I understand that there are only two kinds of people, honest and dishonest. There can be no in-between. You are either one or the other, and whichever one you are, it reflects in your personality.

NAPOLEON HILL:
That's true, and the benefits of honesty are as follows: It establishes a sound basis for confidence; it develops a fundamentally sound and dependable character; it not only attracts people, but it offers opportunities for personal gain in connection with one's occupation. It provides one with a feeling of

self-reliance and self-respect; and it prepares the mind for that power known as faith. A keen sense of honesty discourages avarice, greed, envy, hatred, and selfishness and gives the individual a much better understanding of his rights, privileges, and responsibilities.

ALDERFER:

I understand that there is another important trait that should be included in our broadcast, and that is humility of heart. What about it?

NAPOLEON HILL:

Ah yes, a very important one, inasmuch as arrogance, greed, and egotism are traits that are conspicuous by their absence in the character of a person with this trait. Humility of heart frees one from the influence of these undesirable traits. It is the outgrowth of the understanding of man's relationship to his Creator, plus the recognition that the material blessings of life are gifts from the Creator for the common good of all mankind. The man who is on good terms with his own conscience and in harmony with his Creator is humble of heart, no matter how much of the material riches of life he may have accumulated or what may be his personal achievements.

ALDERFER:

It also seems clear to me that people who lack a general interest in understanding the world in which they live and cannot express themselves satisfactorily are seldom interesting or attractive.

NAPOLEON HILL:

That's true. The statement you just made includes two traits, namely, curiosity and effective speech. The more popular types of people are the more curious type. They have at least a surface knowledge of many subjects, are interested in other people and their ideas, and go out of their way to express that interest where it will inspire appropriate reaction to their own benefit.

He may be curious, but if he cannot stand on his feet and speak with force that connotes an alert and thinking mind, without fear or embarrassment, on any subject of his choice, he is under a great handicap so far as his personality is concerned. The most important factor in effective speech is a thorough knowledge of the subject on which one speaks, and the greatest of all rules of effective speech can be stated in one sentence, "Know what you wish to say, say it with all the emotional feeling you can, then sit down."

ALDERFER:
That's very interesting, because many people fail to follow that last statement, and that is why we have so much confusion in our lives today.

We haven't had time to discuss all of the traits of a pleasing personality, but perhaps we might be able to draw this discussion to a close by telling our audience some of the common habits that destroy attractiveness of personality.

NAPOLEON HILL:
All right, I'll do that. Selfishness, expressed by words, actions, or silent thoughts; sarcasm, expressed by wisecracks that are not so wise; exaggeration, generally due to uncontrolled imagination; an obvious attempt at flattery where it is not justified. Honest praise displeases no one, but be careful not to give it out too freely. Here are others: slovenliness in the posture of the body, in personal adornment, and in speech; endeavoring to convey the impression of superiority through the use of terms and topics with which others are unfamiliar; insincerity, generally expressed through some form of attempted flattery; the habit of finding fault with individuals and the world at large. No one likes a confirmed pessimist, or a know-it-all. The habit of hypochondria, that is, imaginary illness, generally expressed in a vivid description of one's poor health or that of friends and relatives; the habit of belittling those of superior ability, personal attainments, or education; the habit of criticizing that which one does not understand; thoughtlessness, such as turning on a radio full blast and walking away from

the room, leaving it to annoy the neighbors; and the obvious desire for something for nothing.

If you are interested in improving your personality, you should analyze yourself against these common habits that destroy a winning personality. You will find that by eliminating these common habits you will develop into a person who will be liked by others because you have a winning personality.

ALDERFER:
Thank you, Napoleon Hill. This principle discussed today has been a very valuable one, and if our radio audience is interested in making a change for the better, they can do so by conditioning their mind to the idea that all of these personality traits are attainable if they believe them to be so and act upon them with faith applied to their daily living.

Next Sunday we will discuss the principle of Self-Discipline, asking you this question, "Do you have control over yourself and your actions?"

△

WISDOM TO LIVE BY

1. Your personality is the total of the mental, spiritual, and physical traits that distinguish you from all others.

2. It is the factor that determines whether you are liked or disliked by others.

3. It is the medium by which you will negotiate your way through life. It will determine, to a large extent, your ability to associate and cooperate with others with a minimum of friction and opposition.

4. In the traits of a winning personality described by Napoleon Hill you have a measuring device by which you can accurately determine and evaluate your own personality.

5. The financial value of a winning personality may be measured by observing that those who have negative, disagreeable personalities seldom are found in positions of responsibility. They

are not found in the higher income brackets. People with winning personalities have little difficulty selling themselves in all their relationships.

6. Your personality is your greatest asset and can be your greatest liability; *your personality is your trademark.*

ADVERSITY AND ADVANTAGE

Napoleon Hill said that one of the greatest skills needed to succeed is the ability to negotiate with other people without irritating them. This skill provides you with the most important fundamental of leadership in any calling or profession. It establishes harmony within your mind, which is the first requirement for harmony in relationship with others. It is an essential asset for accumulation of all material riches. It embraces everything that controls your mind, your body, and your spirit. It helps convert defeat into victory. No adversity is insurmountable if you acquire all the traits of a winning personality.

▼

CHAPTER 8

SELF-DISCIPLINE
(A MENTAL POWER CLOSE TO DIVINITY)

△

"The man who acquires the ability to take full possession of his own mind may take possession of everything else to which he is justly entitled. And the man who masters himself through self-discipline never can be mastered by others."

Andrew Carnegie

OVERVIEW

Hill explores the incredible power of self-control in this chapter, teaching you how to use self-discipline so that you may never give in to defeat and discouragement.

The purpose of this lesson is to help you find wisdom, happiness, and peace of mind. You will:

- Discover the ways to develop self-control and the benefits it brings

- Become aware of the areas of your life where you need self-control

- Learn to balance the emotions of the heart and the reasoning faculty of your mind

Discovering these aspects about yourself may prove to be a real turning point in your life. Knowing how to develop and practice self-discipline will change your habits forever; you will embark on a path toward fulfillment without the possibility of being run off course, and you will steer steadily toward the life of your dreams.

BROADCAST 8. SELF-DISCIPLINE

ANNOUNCER:

Success Unlimited is on the air, presenting once more the distinguished success philosopher Napoleon Hill, whose success books are now published and distributed as bestsellers in every civilized country, where they have benefitted millions of people. Today Napoleon Hill brings you an idea and makes you a promise that, if you are ready to accept it, can change not only your own life for the better, but it can change as well your entire community or the place where you are occupied in your work, as well as the mental atmosphere of your own home. And now here is Henry Alderfer, associate director of education of the Napoleon Hill Institute, who will assist Napoleon Hill on this program. Mr. Alderfer.

ALDERFER:

Thank you. Today we are going to present the principle of Self-Discipline, or the control of your thoughts and actions. There is no single requirement for individual success as important as self-discipline. It means taking possession of your mind, and here is Napoleon Hill who will outline some of the benefits that will come to you if you learn to master this principle.

NAPOLEON HILL:

Good afternoon, my friends. Yes, Henry, there are a number of benefits you will receive when you master this principle and some of them are: Your imagination will become more alert; your enthusiasm will become keener; your initiative will become more active; your self-reliance will be greater; the scope of your vision will be widened; you will look at the world through different eyes; your personality will become more magnetic; your hopes and ambitions will be stronger; and your faith will be more powerful.

ALDERFER:

That's a good line-up of results, which should satisfy anyone who really practices this principle. When you discipline yourself, you control yourself both in words and deeds. This will result in the control over the emotions, won't it?

NAPOLEON HILL:

Yes it will, and since the emotions are states of mind and are therefore subject to your control and direction, you will be able to use the seven positive emotions, namely, love, sex, hope, faith, enthusiasm, loyalty, and desire, in whatever manner you wish, and you will be able to eliminate or transmute the seven negative emotions, which are fear, jealousy, hatred, revenge, greed, anger, and superstition. You will recognize that emotional control is of increased importance to you when you realize that most people allow emotions to rule their lives, and that these emotions largely rule the world.

ALDERFER:

Habits are automatic acts that we perform daily, either for good or bad. All of us are creatures of habit, aren't we? How do our habits relate to self-discipline?

NAPOLEON HILL:

Self-discipline is a matter of adopting constructive habits. What you really are, what you do, either your failures or your successes, are the results of your habits. Isn't it a blessing then that these habits can be self-made, and the most important habits are those of thought? You will unavoidably and finally display in your deeds the nature of your thought habits. When you have gained control over your thought habits, you will have gone a long way toward the mastery of self-discipline. Definite motives are the beginning of thought habits. Self-discipline without definiteness of motive is impossible, and besides, it would be worthless to you. No one ever achieved anything without a motive.

ALDERFER:

I have heard it said that emotion without reason is man's greatest enemy. Do you agree, and would you explain to our radio listeners exactly what that means?

NAPOLEON HILL:

That's a very interesting statement, and I know that anyone who wishes to succeed must use reason and emotions with a balance of each. Hardly a day passes in anyone's life without him "feeling" like doing something his reason tells him not to do. Both the head-reasoning, and the heart-emotions need a master, and they will find such a master in the faculty of willpower. The ego, acting through the will, acts as a presiding judge only for the person who has deliberately trained his ego for the job through self-discipline. In the absence of this self-discipline, the ego minds its own business and lets reason and emotions fight out their battles as they please, and in this case the man within whose mind the fight is carried on often gets badly hurt.

It is because of this inward conflict, which goes on without a referee, that so many people have problems that they are unable to solve for themselves and that send them running to the psychiatrist. This conflict is one of the basic causes of the increase of neuroses in our culture today. In other words, the need for self-discipline is increasing as our culture becomes more complicated in its demands upon human minds.

ALDERFER:

Very interesting. Before leaving this part of our discussion will you explain to us the fact that not only do we need this self-discipline to control our emotions, but we need it especially in the case of a number of items in life that you believe should be put on the "must control" list.

NAPOLEON HILL:

Yes, that's right. There are four items that appear on this list, namely, our appetite, that is for food and drink; our mental attitude; the use of our time; and definiteness of purpose, and each one of these requires a great deal of self-discipline.

In the case of the first, food and drink, it is a well-established fact that a great many people don't exercise enough discipline in regard to the amount and kinds of food that they put into their body. After a certain point has been reached, in which the actual needed nourishment is supplied to restore body tissues worn out by our physical and mental effort, additional food only imposes an extra strain upon the organs and accumulates a surplus that builds fatty tissue. Too much fat, especially in middle age and after, tends to reduce one's efficiency and to shorten one's life. The same thing holds true with drinking. There is a necessity for controlling your desire for strong drinks, otherwise you are inviting disaster and failure.

ALDERFER:

I notice, Mr. Hill, that this idea of mental attitude appears in this "must" list. It seems that one's mental attitude in regard to everything is extremely important; am I right in this deduction?

NAPOLEON HILL:

You certainly are, because all through life a positive mental attitude is the only frame of mind in which you can have definiteness of a worthwhile purpose and by which you can induce anyone else to cooperate with you and help you to attain it. I think it's very important to remind you that the Creator has given you the right of control over but one thing in all this world, and that's your mental attitude. You can use it negatively to attract all the things you don't want, or by neglecting it you can allow the weeds to take over the garden spot of your mind, or you can pay the price to learn ways of keeping it positive and to attract things you want in life. In other words, your ability to get along with others, which is one of the most important characteristics in the lives of all of us, is determined mainly by your frame of mind or your positive mental attitude.

ALDERFER:

The third one of these "musts" is the proper use of time. So many of us don't realize that the time we spend and the way in which we spend it are extremely important.

NAPOLEON HILL:

That's right, Henry. There's an old saying, "Wasting time is sinful," and it's sad but true. I can't tell you how to spend your time, but I can point out to you that your time is the most precious asset you have. It's like money in the bank if it's used correctly. And like money in the bank, it should be spent under strict self-discipline. Time is funny stuff—you can't save it except by spending it wisely. The average person works eight hours a day. He needs approximately eight hours for sleep, and this leaves another eight hours of "free time" to invest as he pleases. Mark this, Henry, it is the way in which this free time is invested that makes the difference between success and failure in life. Think this over, and make up your mind that you're going to set up a chart for the expenditure of your allotment of twenty-four hours.

ALDERFER:

I have done that, Mr. Hill, and I find that budgeting of time is very important and makes one aware of the amount of time one wastes when it is not budgeted. And it's also interesting to know that the fourth "must," namely, Definiteness of Purpose, fits right in with this use of time.

NAPOLEON HILL:

That's correct, because unless one has a definite goal and a means of attaining it, the problem of what to do with one's time will always arise in one's mind. Self-discipline regarding your definite purpose, that is, setting up this task for yourself, analyzing your capabilities, and then writing down your aims and plans requires a great deal of thought and energy and the disciplining of your ideas to get what you want out of life. It's important to realize that even Infinite Intelligence, as all-powerful as it is, can't help you if you don't make up your mind what it is you want and where you are going.

ALDERFER:

That's very, very interesting, and I think this idea of self-discipline can be made clear to our audience with an illustration or a story. Would you give us one?

NAPOLEON HILL:

Here's one that illustrates the point. There was a man who came to this great country and started out with only a basket—just a twenty-five cent basket—and a handful of bananas. He starts peddling them, and if he sells one, he can eat one during the day. If he doesn't sell one, he can't afford to eat one. By and by, he makes enough to buy a little pushcart. On the cart he has oranges, grapes, and pears in addition to the bananas. First thing you know, he has a little hole-in-the-wall store in a shack somewhere, near a parking lot. Next he leases the lot and builds a building on it. Before you know it, he buys the lot outright and puts up a modern store that does a thriving business. And the next thing we know, he is the head of the largest chain of banks in the world. His name is A.D. Giannini, founder of the Bank of America. All this was possible because he had the Definiteness of Purpose, the Persistence, the Faith, and the Self-Discipline to make what he had fit his needs and goals. You and I are starting from a slightly improved economic level, and we have the benefit of this philosophy, but we, too, must pay the price tag on "Success"!

ALDERFER:
I see what you mean. In order to be successful, one must pay the price, and one can't get something for nothing. If one does, it's not appreciated nearly as much as when he worked for it.

I notice in your own life story, when you were doing twenty years of research on the principles that we are discussing, that you were required to use self-discipline quite a number of times. Would you tell us about it?

NAPOLEON HILL:
There were times in my own experience when I didn't have a friend, not even among my relatives, except my stepmother, and sometimes I wondered if even she wasn't putting on an act. There were times when my opponents said, "He's talking about success, and he doesn't have two nickels to rub together himself." And the worst part of it was, they were right! I put in some twenty years of extreme self-discipline. I had to discipline myself to put up with the initial widespread lack of interest in this developing philosophy. I had to have sufficient self-discipline to carry me through those lean years. No matter who you are, when you first start you will encounter seemingly insurmountable obstacles.

I well remember the first class to which I taught this philosophy. It consisted of six people, and four of them walked out on me the very first day! One of them refused to pay because he said he didn't feel he had received his money's worth, and confidentially, I think maybe he told the truth. You have to have self-discipline to get over those rough spots in the beginning. You have to discipline your tastes and your standard of living and make them fit what you have right now, until the time comes when you have more. The best way to avoid discouragement in the face of adversity is to confide in no one but those who have a genuine sympathy with your cause and an understanding of your possibilities. Otherwise, keep your plans to yourself and let your actions speak. Adopt the motto "Deeds, not words." It's a good motto for all of us.

ALDERFER:

I understand that you owned and operated the first automobile driving school in the United States and personally trained men and women to drive, and in this business of teaching people to drive, you organized three major rules, all of which call for self-discipline. Mr. Hill, with the automobile traffic hazard as great as it is, and with accidents as numerous as they are, and with people being killed or maimed almost every hour of the day, would you give our audience your three rules for driving a car?

NAPOLEON HILL:

I'll be glad to, because I am positive that if drivers will follow these three rules, the death rate and accident toll will be cut considerably. Here they are.

First, I never, under any circumstances, drive faster than will permit me to control the circumstances within the range of my vision—on the right, on the left, behind me, and ahead of me. I keep a sharp lookout all four ways all the time, and no matter what the other motorist does, I manage to have my car safely under control. If you don't think it takes self-discipline to do this, you just get out on a nice stretch of highway where there is nothing in sight for miles, and notice how difficult it is for you to keep your foot off the gas.

Second, I never, under any circumstances, get angry at another motorist or have an argument, even in my own mind, no matter what he does wrong. I will tell you why I demand this of myself. The minute you get mad, you don't have control of your car, and you have no business on the highway, because a car not under control is a lethal weapon. Most people who have accidents are worried or afraid or angry and do not have a positive attitude. Anybody driving without a positive attitude is in danger. He doesn't see four ways. He is lucky if he sees one way. It takes self-discipline not to argue with the other fellow.

Third, I never, under any circumstances, take an avoidable hazard when I am driving on the road. By a hazard I mean the chance you take when you try to steal a split second in making a light or trying to run around a curve where you cannot see ahead. It is a hazard to take any chance just to save two or three seconds. In other words, I agree with the fellow who said he'd rather be five minutes late over here than twenty years early "over there."

ALDERFER:

Wonderful, these are simple rules, and yet I venture to say that all accidents today are due to the violation of one or more of them. It's true, the other motorist doesn't control the situation, you do, and if you start using your self-discipline, you will help to make our highways safer.

I think this leads right into self-discipline in the relationship to others, and you have a story that illustrates this very well. Would you tell our audience about it?

NAPOLEON HILL:

I will be glad to. In my younger days I used to go around not only with a chip on my shoulder, but a whole block of wood and a sign up there that said, "I dare you to knock it off." And somebody did always come along and knock it off, too! As I acquired self-discipline, I took down the sign. It helped some, but not enough. I found I had to reduce the block to a chip, which helped some more. Finally, I said to myself: "I will have a shoulder that is fully free, with no chip for anyone to knock off." I stopped expecting people to find fault, and lo and behold! The world around me began to change from one of disharmony to one of harmony and cooperation. I changed the world I lived in simply by changing my own mental attitude.

At one time I didn't like people who wore loud, flashy clothes. Do you know how I overcame that? I started wearing them myself to see how I would feel. In other words, by getting the other fellow's viewpoint, I found that under the same circumstances, my reaction was much the same as theirs. When you get into that positive frame of mind and quit disliking people just because they're different from you, you will find this a more friendly world in which to live. If you want to get people to see your way or to cooperate with you, do your part first by getting into the right frame of mind to attract them.

You'll be astonished at how quickly they will change their attitude toward you. This matter of self-discipline can be made to serve a lot of purposes.

ALDERFER:

Self-discipline is the procedure by which one coordinates the mind or, more clearly stated, the six departments of the mind that you have identified in your books, so that none of them gets out of control. What are these six departments of the mind that are subject to control by the individual?

NAPOLEON HILL:

The six divisions or departments of the mind that are subject to control by the individual are 1) The Ego—This is the seat of the willpower and acts as a Supreme Court, with the power to reverse, modify, change, or eliminate altogether the entire work of all the other departments of the mind. 2) The Faculty of the Emotions—Here is generated the driving force that sets one's thoughts, plans, and purposes into action. 3) The Faculty of Reason—This is where one may weigh, estimate, and properly evaluate the products of the imagination and of the emotions. 4) The Faculty of Imagination—This is where one may create ideas, plans, and methods of attaining desired ends. 5) The Conscience—This is where one may test the moral worth of one's thoughts, plans, and purposes. 6) The Memory—This serves as the keeper of records of all experiences and as a filing cabinet for all sense perceptions and the inspiration of Infinite Intelligence. When these departments of the mind are coordinated and properly guided by self-discipline, they enable a person to negotiate his way through life with a minimum of opposition from others.

ALDERFER:

I understand that the ego, which is the seat of willpower, must remain strong. How does one keep it that way? Can you tell us?

NAPOLEON HILL:

Yes, I'll explain it in reference to myself, but every one of you can do the same with your own ego. I will describe the three imaginary walls of outer defense I keep around the ego I know as Napoleon Hill. Starting with the outside one, and working in, the first wall is just high enough to keep away from me the people who really have no business getting to me to take up my time. This outer wall has several doors in it, and it is not too difficult to enter one of them. If a person can establish a reasonable right to my time, I open one of the doors and let him in, but he has to establish that right.

The next wall is very much taller, and there is only one door in it, which I watch very closely. The number of persons who get in through that door is comparatively smaller. Before the door swings open to admit anyone, he must have established the fact that he has something that I want, or that we have something in common that will be mutually helpful.

The third and final wall is so tall that no person in the world, except my Creator, has ever scaled it, and there are no doors in it whatsoever. Not even my own wife is ever allowed inside that wall, because it surrounds and protects the ego of Napoleon Hill. Let me tell you that if you are going to open the door of your ego and personality and let anyone who chooses walk in and out, they will take away a lot of things that you won't want them to have. I admonish you to throw a protective wall around your own mind. Have a place where you can retire to yourself, where you can commune with Infinite Intelligence.

ALDERFER:

In your explanation of the ego, you have given us the source of our will-power, which controls our reasoning. But reason isn't the only fact over which we must exercise control. What about the emotions? What do we do about those?

NAPOLEON HILL:

This so-called second division of the mind, the faculty of emotions, is very important because of the necessity for balancing the emotions or feelings of the heart with the faculty of reason to make a satisfactory solution possible. And there is another aspect of the emotions that I would like to consider because it concerns problems that arise in one's mind in connection with disappointments and failures and the broken hearts that occur as the result of the loss of material things or the loss of friends or loved ones. Self-discipline is the only real solution for such problems.

Discipline begins with the recognition of the fact that there are only two kinds of problems: one, those you can solve, and two, those you can't solve. The problems that you can solve should be immediately cleared up by the most practical means available, and those that have no solution should be put out of your mind and forgotten. Self-discipline, which means the mastery over all the emotions, can close the door between yourself and all unpleasing experiences of the past. You must close the door tightly and lock it securely, so there is no possibility of its being opened again. Those who lack self-discipline often stand in the doorway and look wistfully backward into the past instead of closing the door and looking forward into the future. There can be no compromise with this door-closing business. You must place the power of your will against the door that shuts out the things you wish to forget, and this requires self-discipline.

ALDERFER:

Now I'm beginning to understand what you mean. Self-discipline closes the door tightly against all manner of fears and opens wide the door to hope and faith. It closes the door tightly against jealousy and opens wide a new door to love. Self-discipline looks forward, not backward. It blocks out discouragement and worry; it encourages the positive emotions and keeps out the negative emotions. It is developed for the purpose of making your mind strong; it enables you to take possession of your own mind and control your own mental attitude. You cannot have real self-discipline until you can organize your mind and keep it clear of all disturbing influences. Is that a pretty good summary?

NAPOLEON HILL:

Yes, it is. Before we close today I would like to give our audience my creed for self-discipline, as follows: "Ego, the seat of willpower: Recognizing that the Power of Will is the Supreme Court over all other departments of my mind, I will exercise it daily to be prepared when I need an urge to action for any purpose; and I will form habits designed to bring the power of my will into action at least once daily. Emotions: Realizing that my emotions are both positive and negative, I will form daily habits that will encourage the development of the positive emotions and aid me in the converting of the negative emotions into some form of useful action. Reason: Recognizing that both my positive emotions and my negative emotions may be dangerous if they are not controlled and directed to desirable ends, I will be guided by my reason in giving expression to these. Imagination: Recognizing the need for sound plans and ideas for the attainment of my desires, I will develop my imagination by calling upon it daily for help in the formation of my plans. Conscience: Recognizing that my emotions often err in their overenthusiasm, and my faculty of reason often is without the warmth of feeling that is necessary to enable me to combine justice with mercy in my judgments, I will encourage my conscience to guide me as to what is right and what is wrong, and I will never set aside the verdicts it renders, no matter what may be the cost of carrying them out. Memory: Recognizing the value of an alert memory, I will encourage mine to become alert by taking care to impress it clearly with all thoughts I wish to recall, and by associating those thoughts with related subjects that I may call to mind frequently. Subconscious mind: Recognizing the influence of my subconscious mind over my willpower, I shall take care to submit to it a clear and definite picture of my goal in life and all minor purposes leading to my goal, and I shall keep this picture constantly before my subconscious mind by repeating it daily."

ALDERFER:

Those are very powerful ideas that you have discussed, and one of the faculties that intrigues me very much is that of conscience. Would you tell us a little more about our conscience?

NAPOLEON HILL:

The conscience is the faculty that rules upon the moral quality of your actions and motives. If your conscience is always consulted and the counsel is always obeyed, it is a valuable aid. If it is neglected or ignored and insulted by neglect of its advice, it will become an offender and a conspirator. When this occurs, it is time to take heed, because society has had to build a lot of special rooms for people who have let this happen, and the view from these rooms is always obstructed by bars.

A man may deny his conscience momentarily, but the day will come when this conscience that has been denied or subdued will turn with fury and torment him all through his waking life and also during his sleep at night. There is nothing that will arouse fear as quickly as hidden guilt. And if one examines his own conscience, it brings to the surface those hidden faults and the means of discovering the things that are destroying and choking off one's peace of mind. Every person has a little corner in his soul into which he doesn't wish anyone to look. The short phrase "Let your conscience be your guide" is of great importance, because if your reason says yes and your conscience says no, follow your conscience.

ALDERFER:

Thank you, Napoleon Hill for the excellent description of our conscience and how it affects our lives, and for your explanation of how we learn to control ourselves by using self-discipline. I know our audience has gained a great deal of help from this discussion.

Please join us next Sunday afternoon, radio friends, when Napoleon Hill will discuss the importance of a Positive Mental Attitude to attaining one's goals in life.

△

WISDOM TO LIVE BY

1. It is critically important to understand that the only thing over which you have complete control is your own mental attitude.

2. The desire for freedom of mind and body and the desire for riches are universal desires, but few attain them because they don't recognize that the real source of both is in their own minds.

3. Deliberately place in your own mind the sort of thoughts that you desire there and keep out of your mind thoughts that you don't desire, and you will become a person with self-control.

4. Through self-discipline you may think yourself into or out of any circumstance of life. Self-discipline will help you to control your mental attitude. Your mental attitude may help you to master every circumstance of your life and convert every adversity, every defeat, and every failure into an asset of equivalent scope.

5. Self-control is mind control. Mind control is the result of self-discipline and habit. You either control your mind or it controls you. There is no compromise.

6. The most practical method for controlling your mind is the habit of keeping it busy with a definite purpose backed by a definite plan.

7. The major function of self-discipline is to maintain proper balance between the judgment of the mind and the sentiments of the heart.

8. Hill says, "Let your own conscience be your guide." If your reason says yes and your conscience says no, follow your conscience.

ADVERSITY AND ADVANTAGE

Our fears, our limitations, our superstitions, and our negative state of mind bring us failure and adversity. As we have learned, when we start searching for a seed of equal or better benefit in any adversity, we also develop self-discipline, which opens the doors to hope, faith, love, positive emotions, good health, sense of purpose, constructive habits, and much more. Without adversity we would never know or discover these traits.

▼

CHAPTER 9

POSITIVE MENTAL ATTITUDE

(A BLESSING OF THE HIGHEST ORDER)

"No pessimist ever discovered the secret of the stars, or
sailed to an uncharted land, or opened a new doorway
for the human spirit."

Helen Keller

OVERVIEW

The purpose of this chapter is to introduce you to the concept that a positive mental attitude is essential to obtaining positive outcomes, and consequently is necessary to achieve success.

Hill will reveal to you:

- A state of mind that brings you wealth, peace of mind and good health. This state of mind helps you become immune against all fears and self-imposed limitations.

- A single cause in human nature that has destroyed more people than any other cause

- A way to break undesirable habits

- The source to connect to Infinite Intelligence

You can train yourself to have a positive mental attitude using the lesson in this chapter. This critical ability to habitually think positively will reap benefits that will propel you on your journey toward a lifetime of success.

BROADCAST 9. A POSITIVE MENTAL ATTITUDE

ANNOUNCER:

Good afternoon, ladies and gentlemen. The Radio School of Success Unlimited is on the air. Today's lesson in the Science of Success will be given by Napoleon Hill. His Radio School of Success Unlimited can be a great help to you—if you'll just let it. Now, Napoleon Hill and his associate Henry Alderfer.

ALDERFER:

Thank you. Today we are going to present the success principle that we will call a "Positive Mental Attitude." With a positive mental attitude we can put our mind to work believing in success as our right, and our belief will guide us directly toward whatever goal we wish to achieve. We will discuss the meaning of a positive mental attitude, and here is Napoleon Hill to tell us all about it and to outline the benefits that you will receive when you learn to master this principle. Napoleon Hill.

NAPOLEON HILL:

Good afternoon, my friends. Yes, Henry, this principle of a Positive Mental Attitude is so rich in significance that it may affect our entire lives, and because of this, we will analyze it carefully.

ALDERFER:

I understand that at the time of our birth, each of us brings with him the equivalent of two sealed envelopes, in one of which appears a list of riches we may enjoy by taking possession of our own minds and using them for the attainment of what we desire in life, and in the other appears a list of penalties that Nature will exact from us if we neglect to recognize and use our mind power.

NAPOLEON HILL:

That's right, and we will break the seal of these two envelopes and present you with their contents. But more important than that, I suggest that you discover for yourself that these sealed envelopes are not imaginary, but real, and that they may be the means of putting you on the success beam on which you can ride to victory and to a destination of your own choosing. But I want to warn you that you will not get the full meaning of this principle unless you are ready to receive it and put it to use.

There is one thing that Nature definitely discourages and penalizes severely, namely, a vacuum, that is, emptiness and idleness, lack of activity. Remove from active use any muscle of your body, and it will atrophy and become useless. The same thing holds true for your mind. If you don't use it for constructive purposes, the weeds of failure will spring up and take over.

ALDERFER:

I see what you mean. You either use your brain for controlled thinking in connection with things you want, or Nature steps in and uses it to grow you a bountiful crop of negative circumstances you don't want. And you have a choice in this connection; you can take possession of your thought power or you can let it be influenced by all the stray winds of chance and circumstances you don't desire. You can make your mind focus on positive thinking or you can let it drift to negative thinking, but you can't sit idly by and thereby free yourself from the influence of these two sealed envelopes.

NAPOLEON HILL:

That's correct. Remember, whatever you have, you use it or you lose it. You either embrace the sealed envelope marked "riches" and follow its instructions or you are forced to suffer the penalties in the other envelope. Out of this truth has grown the saying "success attracts more success, while failure attracts more failure," a truth that we have observed many times, although few of us have analyzed the cause behind it. Nature allows you to fix your mind on whatever you desire and create your own plan for attaining it.

ALDERFER:

That's becoming very clear to me now, and I understand why success attracts more success once you have placed yourself on the success beam, and it's also equally clear why failure attracts more failure if by neglect you haven't taken possession of your mind and put it to work. Now let's break down the contents of these two sealed envelopes and see what they contain. Will you open the one labeled "riches" or "rewards" first and tell us the blessings this one will bring?

NAPOLEON HILL:

Fine. You know, Henry, if you have a positive mental attitude, that is, if you think positively, you will have the following blessings. First, you will have the privilege of placing yourself on the success beam, which attracts only the circumstances that make for success; second, you will have sound health, both physical and mental; third, you will become independent financially; fourth, you will engage in a labor of love by which you may fully express yourself; fifth, you will have peace of mind; sixth, you will have faith, which makes fear impossible; seventh, you will have lasting friends; eighth, you will live a long and well-balanced life; ninth, you will be immune against all fears and self-limitations; and tenth, you will have wisdom with which to understand yourself and others.

ALDERFER:

It's very encouraging to realize that these wonderful blessings are available to us if we make up our minds to accept them. The other envelope, labeled "penalties," has a number of ingredients. What are they?

NAPOLEON HILL:

This particular list is just the opposite of the blessings you could receive. First, your actions will attract only poverty and misery all of your life; second, you will have mental and physical ailments of many kinds; third, you will never reach financial independence and will always look to others for help, or you will simply drift; fourth, you will dislike lowly occupations from which you will earn what little is available to you; fifth, you will experience every brand of worry known to mankind; sixth, you will have faith in no one and nothing and will suffer from relentless fears; seventh, you will have many enemies and few, if any, friends; eighth, your life will be beset with worry and will be cut short; ninth, your life will be overcome with doubt and lack of self-confidence; and tenth, you will lack any understanding of why your life has been wasted.

ALDERFER:

So that's the catalog of our riches and penalties, and I understand you must embrace one or have the other forced upon you. There is no halfway point, no means of compromise. You are on trial as a citizen of life and are the judge and the jury, the attorney for the defense and the prosecutor, and the final verdict is what happens to you through your life because of your mental attitude.

You have described these riches and penalties. Can you tell us now just how important is a positive mental attitude to obtaining these riches?

NAPOLEON HILL:

There are quite a number of benefits to be derived from a positive mental attitude, but time doesn't allow us to give all of them, so we will confine our discussion to the most important ones. A positive mental attitude is the first and most important step we must take in the control and direction of our minds, since all degrees of a negative mental attitude leave us wide open to every adverse influence we come in contact with. It's the only condition of the mind with which we can give ourselves complete protection against all fears and sources of worry. It's the only condition of the mind in which we can express Applied Faith and draw upon the forces of Infinite Intelligence at will, and therefore, it's the foundation on which all prayers should be expressed. It's the only condition of the mind in which we can meet and recognize our Other Self—that self which has no self-limitations and always remains in our possession if we direct it to desired ends. And it's the only condition of our mind that permits us to write our own ticket in life and be sure of making life pay off in dividends of our own choosing.

ALDERFER:

I understand then, from all of these statements, that a positive mental attitude is the only condition of the mind in which we can gain the wisdom with which to recognize the true purpose of life and adapt ourselves to that purpose. In other words, a positive mental attitude is a must for all who want to make life pay off on their own terms.

You have told us how important a positive mental attitude is; that is, you have told us why. Now please tell us how; that is, the steps we can take to develop a positive mental attitude.

NAPOLEON HILL:

It's always important when you talk about a thing, especially if you say how important it is, to give ways of developing it, and here are some of the ways in which you can produce this frame of mind. First, you can recognize your privilege of taking possession of your own mind as being the one and only thing over which you have complete control. This realization is a necessary step before you can benefit by any of the succeeding ones. You can then recognize and prove to your own satisfaction the truth that every adversity, every failure, every defeat, every heartbreak, every unpleasing circumstance of your own making or otherwise, carries with it the seed of an equivalent advantage that may be transmuted or changed into a blessing of great proportions.

ALDERFER:

I understand also that it will be necessary for us to learn to close the door behind us on all the failures and unpleasant circumstances that we have experienced in the past, thus clearing the way for that frame of mind called a positive mental attitude. And I also note that you can find out what you desire most in life and begin getting it right where you now are by helping as many others as possible to acquire similar benefits, thus putting into action that magic success principle, the habit of Going the Extra Mile.

NAPOLEON HILL:

That's correct, Henry, and you can determine how much material wealth you require. Set up a plan for acquiring it, and then place a stopgap on your emotions, to be registered by adopting the principle of not too much and not too little, by which to guide your future ambitions for material things. Greed for an overabundance of material things has destroyed more people than any other single cause. And you can form the habit of saying or doing something each day that will make other people feel better, even if it's nothing more than making a telephone call or dropping them a postcard.

ALDERFER:

These illustrations you are giving are how to take possession of one's mind so that it will express a positive mental attitude automatically at all times.

You in our radio audience can do it by finding out what you like best to do. Discover a labor of love and do it with all your heart and soul, even if it's only a hobby. And you can learn that when you meet with a personal problem, the solution of which you have tried to find without success, if you will look around and find someone with a similar or even greater problem and help them to find the solution, by the time theirs has been found, yours will be revealed to you.

NAPOLEON HILL:

You can also take a complete inventory of other assets you possess, exclusive of material riches, and discover that your greatest asset is a sound mind with which you can shape your own destiny by the simple process of taking full possession of it and directing it to ends of your own choosing. You will recognize that the space you occupy in this world is in exact ratio to the quality and the quantity of the service you render for the benefit of others plus the mental attitude in which you render it.

ALDERFER:

I understand too, that with a positive mental attitude, if you have objectionable habits that you desire to break, you can show yourself who is boss by refraining from those habits for a period of one month. After that, there will be no doubt as to who is in control of your mind. And you can remember always that no one can hurt your feelings or make you angry or frightened without your full cooperation and consent.

NAPOLEON HILL:

And you can use your own mind in shaping your own destiny to fit whatever purposes in life you choose and thereby avail yourself of all the riches that are due you, and you can keep your mind so busy doing things you like to do that there will be no time left to stray off after things you don't want or like to do. And you can attune your mind to attract to you the things and circumstances you wish by expressing in a daily prayer your feeling of gratitude for having received the blessings that you desire.

ALDERFER:

A good way to maintain a positive mental attitude is to keep a diary of your good deeds and never let the sun set on any single day without performing and recording some act of human kindness. The benefits of this habit will be cumulative and eventually will give you a high place in the hearts of your fellow man. And let us remember that one good deed each day will keep old man gloom away.

NAPOLEON HILL:

We are still discussing ways and means of conditioning our minds to become and remain positive, but it must seem obvious that this conditioning process has many methods of approach that leave no room for alibis for not establishing a positive mental attitude. You will find the steps we listed for you will lead to a positive mental attitude and give you everything you need to help you acquire this desirable asset. You can recognize the truth that there is no existing personal problem that has no solution. There are adequate solutions for all problems, although the best solutions for your problem may not be those you have chosen or would prefer.

Think of the problems that Thomas Edison had with his handicap of only three months of formal schooling; or Helen Keller, with her affliction of the lack of sight and hearing; or Milo C. Jones with his double paralysis, which deprived him of the use of his body but made him realize he had a mind that he could use to develop the "little pig sausages"; or Henry Ford, with his limited schooling and the derision of his relatives and neighbors who believed him to be mentally off balance because his major purpose was to change the American way of life and create the vast Ford empire as we know it today. There are many more individuals that could be mentioned who had a positive mental attitude despite major handicaps, but time doesn't permit.

ALDERFER:

A positive mental attitude is needed by people to discover the difference between wishing and believing and acting for the attainment of their desires.

You have said there are six steps in this mind power attainment that the majority of people need to recognize. Will you please tell our audience what they are?

NAPOLEON HILL:

I'll be glad to. A great many people never discover the difference between wishing and believing, and they are the largest part of our population. First, the vast majority of people, about 70 percent, go all through life by merely wishing for things. Second, a much smaller percentage, about 10 percent, develop their wishes into desires. Third, a still smaller percentage, 8 percent, develop their wishes and desires into hopes, and a still smaller percentage, about 6 percent, step up their mind power to where their wishes, their desires, and hopes become beliefs; and still a very much smaller percentage, 4 percent, of the people crystallize their wishes, desires, and hopes into belief and then into a burning desire, and finally faith. And last, the smallest percentage of all, 2 percent, take the last two critical steps by putting their faith into action by planning and acting. These are the builders of civilization!

ALDERFER:

In other words, the latter class, the 2 percent group, are the great successes in every calling. They are the Andrew Carnegies, the Henry Fords, the Thomas Edisons, the Alexander Graham Bells, the Rockefellers, and the leaders in every walk of life. They are the people who recognize the power of their own mind and take possession of that power and direct it to whatever ends they choose. To these people the word "impossible" has no meaning. To them, everything they want or need is possible, and they manage to get it. These are the builders of empires, the advancers of civilization and the leaders of all callings in every nation on earth. And the only trait that distinguishes them from most of the others, who accept failure, is that they recognize and use their mind power for the attainment of the circumstances they want.

You have told us about the different groups of people and the percentage of those in the last group. Now how does one get into that 2 percent class of those successful people? Would you tell us how?

NAPOLEON HILL:

Yes, it's very important, Henry, and here are two suggestions that are vitally important to those who sincerely desire to achieve the things they want out of life. First, you must adjust yourself to other people's states of mind and their peculiarities so as to get along peacefully with them. Refrain from taking notice of the trivial circumstances in your relationship and refuse to allow them to become controversial incidents.

Second, establish your own technique for conditioning your mind at the start of each day so you can maintain a positive mental attitude throughout the day.

ALDERFER:

I also understand that the habit of adopting a hearty laugh is a fine means of changing anger into a harmless emotion, and it will very effectively change your mind from negative to positive.

NAPOLEON HILL:

That's right, and master salesmen follow this habit daily as a means of conditioning their minds with a positive mental attitude, which is so essential in the work of selling. You must also concentrate your mind on the "can do" portion of all tasks you undertake, and don't worry about the "can't do" portion unless and until it meets you face-to-face. Learn to look upon life as a continuous process of learning from experience, both the good and the bad, and be always on the alert for gains in wisdom that come a little at a time, day by day, through both the pleasant and the unpleasant experiences.

Be careful of your associates because the negative mental attitude of other people is very contagious and it rubs off a little at a time. Remember also that you have a dual personality, one that is positive and has a great capacity for belief, and the other that is negative and has an equally great capacity for disbelief. Put yourself on the side of the personality that believes, and the other personality will disappear because of the lack of exercise.

ALDERFER:

We must also remember that prayer brings the best results when the one who is praying has sufficient faith to see himself already in possession of that for which he prays. This is a positive mental attitude of the highest order, and peace of mind can be attained only by a positive mental attitude.

NAPOLEON HILL:

That's correct, and peace of mind is considered by many to be the highest blessing that life provides. Here are some of the positives that come from peace of mind. First, it gives a complete mastery over all forms of worry; it is freedom from fear in all its forms; it is an escape from feelings of inadequacy; it is the habit of doing one's own thinking on all subjects; it is the habit of helping others to help themselves; it is the recognition of the truth that the universal power of Infinite Intelligence is available to all who will learn to appropriate and use it; it is the joy of getting happiness from doing rather than from possessing; and it is the privilege of engaging in a labor of love of one's own choice.

ALDERFER:

I understand that a positive mental attitude is invaluable to men and women in sales organizations if they are engaged either in selling or in directing the actions of sales people. The attitude in which they do it will be the means by which they can greatly increase their production.

NAPOLEON HILL:

That's right, and we must remember too that all improvement we inspire in the mental attitude of others must begin by improvement in our own mental attitude; this causes like to attract like. Remember too that all sales are made first to the salesman himself by thoroughly conditioning his mind so that it is positive and so that he will believe in that which he is trying to sell.

In all selling, there are two factors of major importance: first, complete analysis by the salesman of the person or persons who are to do the buying, to make sure that the commodity or service being offered for sale is suited to the needs of the buyer or buyers; and second, the tactful planting in the mind of the buyer or buyers of an adequate motive to inspire a purchase. Throughout the transaction the most important thing the salesman has to do is to keep his mind positive and use the sort of language that will convey this state of mind to his prospective buyer.

ALDERFER:

I understand then there is a close relationship in technique between salesmanship and prayer; and that all prayers which are expressed when one is in a state of fear or doubt will result only in negative results; and that only prayers which are expressed with perfect faith and belief in their fulfillment will bring positive results. Note what happens when you believe in that which you are trying to sell to another, when you know it fits his needs, and when you are determined to maintain your contact with the buyer until he accepts your belief and acts upon it.

NAPOLEON HILL:

This brings us to a subject that can't be omitted from this principle of a positive mental attitude, because it will make clear the medium by which your mind communicates both your negative and your positive state. It is known as the subconscious section of the mind. One side of your subconscious faculty connects with your conscious mind, and the opposite side connects with Infinite Intelligence.

Andrew Carnegie once said, "Study any person who is known to be a success, and you will find that he has a definite major goal; he has a plan for the attainment of his goal; and he devotes the major portion of his thoughts and his efforts to the attainment of this purpose. My own purpose," he said, "is that of making and marketing steel. I conceived that purpose while working as a laborer. It became an obsession with me. I took it to bed with me at night, and I took it to work with me in the morning. My definite purpose became more than a mere wish; it became my burning desire, and that is the only sort of definite purpose which seems to bring results." In those words Mr. Carnegie sums up how he used his subconscious mind, the medium through which he translated his burning desire into a huge industrial empire.

All riches and all material things that anyone acquires through his own efforts begin in the form of a clear and concise mental picture of the thing one seeks. When that picture grows or has been forced to the proportions of an obsession, it is taken over by the subconscious mind through some hidden law of nature that the wisest of men do not fully understand. From that point on, one is drawn, attracted, or guided in the direction of the physical equivalent of the mental picture because of a positive mental attitude.

ALDERFER:

Thank you, Napoleon Hill, for a fine discussion of this principle of a Positive Mental Attitude, what it is, how it can be attained, and how we can benefit by its results. Next week we will discuss another subject in the School of the Air that will be of great importance to our listeners, the Twelve Great Riches of Life. Please join us again next Sunday afternoon.

△

WISDOM TO LIVE BY

1. What is a positive mental attitude (PMA)?

    a. It is the right mental attitude in any given situation.

    b. It is a confident, constructive, sure, practical, and forward-moving disposition of the mind over and against any given set of circumstances.

    c. It is composed of the positive characteristics symbolized by words such as faith, integrity, hope, optimism, courage, initiative, generosity, tolerance, tact, kindliness, and good common sense.

2. With a PMA your belief will guide you toward your definite major purpose, whereas a negative mental attitude will fill your thoughts with frustration and fear, and your mind will attract all these penalties. If you make no attempt to control your mind, you will

make it open wide to every negative influence with which you come in contact.

3. Nothing great has ever been achieved without the aid of a positive mental attitude, which begins with a definite major purpose, which is activated by a burning desire, and intensified until the desire becomes applied faith.

ADVERSITY AND ADVANTAGE

1. Thoughts are like magnets. Negative thoughts attract negative circumstances; positive thoughts attract positive outcomes.

2. You may discover that your pattern of negative thinking began early in childhood. The main reason negativity is so common is the belief that life is a struggle, that it is hard and full of problems. Many parents tell or model to their children that life is hard, and the children believe it. It is part of our "problem-solving" cultural bias, where we reward each other for solving problems. Instead of problems, why don't we see opportunities?

3. Train yourself to look for the seed of equivalent benefit in every disappointment you face, and you will see lot of opportunities. Negative thinking costs you mentally, physically, emotionally, and spiritually. Positive thinking pays heavy dividends. *Maintain a positive outlook; things will always work out!*

▼

CHAPTER 10

THE TWELVE GREAT RICHES

(PATHWAY TO PEACE OF MIND)

"Those who acquire money in large amounts without acquiring the other eleven Great Riches do not use the money wisely, and often it turns out that they paid dearly for their monetary riches."

Napoleon Hill

OVERVIEW

In this lesson, Hill's purpose is to make you understand that there are other intangible riches of greater value than money, without which you really cannot have peace of mind, no matter how much money you possess.

In this chapter, Hill discusses:

- The hidden power everyone is born with

- One thing within you that will help you bring harmony with family, coworkers, neighbors, strangers, and above all with the Creator

- What it will take to become the richest person with peace of mind

- The highest form of self-discipline that is necessary for all to succeed

- One fact that will keep you going all the time

- The basis of all miracles

- How to become free and independent

- A way to keep all riches

Millions of people have learned how to find the peace they are seeking by embracing the value of these intangible riches alongside the quest for material wealth. You too can obtain peace of mind with the knowledge contained in this chapter.

BROADCAST 10. THE TWELVE GREAT RICHES

ALDERFER:

Today's program was inspired by the writer of a letter who asked a question we shall answer because you, too, will like to hear the answer. The writer said, "I listen to your program every Sunday, and I am thrilled by it, but there is one question I wish you would answer. When you speak of success and riches, just what do you mean? Of what do riches consist, money, or what?" Our entire program will be devoted to answering this question, and here is Napoleon Hill who will give you the answers.

NAPOLEON HILL:

Good afternoon, my radio friends. To begin with let me explain that there are Twelve Great Riches, or twelve different factors that make one rich, and you will be happy to observe that each of these is something that anyone may acquire very easily.

ALDERFER:

Before Napoleon Hill names the Twelve Great Riches, may I suggest that you write them down as he names them and then analyze yourself carefully to see how many of them you already possess? And now, Mr. Hill, perhaps you will tell our radio audience whether or not one must possess all twelve of these factors before one can be considered rich?

NAPOLEON HILL:

Yes, to be rich in mind, body, and spirit one must possess all twelve of the things that add up to riches, but inasmuch as each of the twelve can be easily acquired by almost anyone, there is but little reason for anyone's remaining poor.

ALDERFER:

And this applies to everyone of every race and every creed, and regardless of one's education or political and religious affiliations. Now, friends, please have your paper and pencil handy, and Napoleon Hill will begin by describing number one of the Twelve Great Riches.

NAPOLEON HILL:

Number one of the Twelve Great Riches is a Positive Mental Attitude. All riches, of whatever nature, begin as a state of mind; and let us remember that your state of mind is the one and only thing over which you have complete, absolute, and unchallengeable control. You can best judge the value of this right to control and direct your own mind by remembering that it is a gift of the Creator by which man was provided with the means by which he may control his earthly destiny and make of it whatever he pleases.

ALDERFER:

By this you mean that man has the privilege of embracing the power of his own mind and directing it to the attainment of everything he desires; or if he neglects to do so and allows his mental attitude to become negative, he will have to accept from life circumstances and things he may not desire.

NAPOLEON HILL:

That is correct. Man's power to control and direct his own mind to ends of his own choice is his greatest asset, and if he embraces this power and directs it through a positive mental attitude, he will attract all of the other eleven factors that make one rich. A positive mental attitude is important because it attracts to one the things and circumstances one desires, whereas a negative mental attitude attracts the things and circumstances one does not desire. I have mentioned this fact in prior broadcasts, but it is so important, it bears repeating.

ALDERFER:

Perhaps you would like to mention some of the desirable things that one may acquire by keeping the mental attitude positive.

NAPOLEON HILL:

A positive mental attitude attracts the riches of true friendship. And the riches one finds in the hope of future achievement. And the riches to be found in a labor of one's own choice, where one may give expression to the highest plane of one's soul. And the riches of one's home, business, and occupational relationships. And the riches of freedom from fear and worry. And the riches of song and laughter. And the riches of enduring faith in Infinite Intelligence, which place one in harmony with the laws of the universe. Yes, these and all other riches begin with a positive mental attitude. Is it any wonder, therefore, that a positive mental attitude takes first place in the list of the Twelve Great Riches?

ALDERFER:

From what you have just been saying, we might be justified if we said that the person who follows the habit of expressing himself through a positive mental attitude is truly the "Master of his fate, the Captain of his own soul," as Henley stated in his poem *Invictus*.

And now we are ready for a description of the second of the Twelve Great Riches.

NAPOLEON HILL:

Number two is Sound Physical Health. Sound health begins with a sound health consciousness, and this is produced by a mind that is positive, a mind that thinks in terms of sound health and not in terms of illness. The hypochondriac—that is, one who suffers with imaginary illness—makes himself ill by the expression of a negative mental attitude.

ALDERFER:

Are we to conclude from what you have said that a positive mental attitude is the only factor with which we may maintain sound health?

NAPOLEON HILL:

No, it isn't the only factor, it is just the most important, because it is literally true that "As a man thinketh in his own heart so is he." And this applies to health and all other factors that affect one's life. Believe you will have sound health, and you will follow sensible habits that will lead to sound health. Believe you will be successful, and you will do the things that will make you successful. You see, when an all-wise Creator gave us complete control over but one thing, our own mind, he knew that with this power of the mind we could create or attract to us everything we might desire or need.

ALDERFER:

Isn't it marvelous when we recognize that we were born with all we need with which to acquire everything we desire? And isn't it shocking to recognize how few people ever discover this hidden power within them?

And now we are ready for number three of the Twelve Riches of Life.

NAPOLEON HILL:

Number three is Harmony in Human Relationships. Harmony with others begins with harmony with one's self. For it is true that there are profound benefits available to those who comply with Shakespeare's admonition "To thine own self be true, and it must follow, as the night the day, thou canst not then be false to any man." After one develops the habit of harmony within himself, he will then find it easy to relate himself harmoniously to his Creator, the members of his family, his associates in his occupation, his neighbors, and the strangers with whom he meets. Harmony within one's self attracts the circumstances and things and people one desires. Disharmony drives these away and attracts the things one does not desire.

ALDERFER:

How can we judge whether or not another person is blessed with the habit of harmony within himself?

NAPOLEON HILL:

Very easily. The person who lacks harmony within himself is nervous; irritable; he speaks with a harsh tone of voice; he seldom if ever smiles; the expression of his face is hard and repulsive; his mannerisms are unfriendly; his habits in general are not dependable; and he throws off a vibration of discomfort and unpleasantness that everyone around him may pick up; hence he is not sought after as a companion or to fill responsible positions; he has a quick, uncontrollable temper; and his acts are apt to be of the selfish type.

ALDERFER:

Well, outside of all this, he may be a very pleasant fellow, may he not? (*Laughingly*)

This brings us to the fourth of the Twelve Great Riches.

NAPOLEON HILL:

Number four is Freedom from Fear. No person who fears anything is a free and independent person such as the Creator intended that all of us should be. Fear is the tool of the evil forces of the world, and you may be sure that wherever this carrion crow hovers, there is something dead that should be buried. The seven most common fears that curse mankind are the fear of poverty, the fear of criticism, the fear of ill health, the fear of loss of love of someone, the fear of loss of liberty, the fear of old age, and the fear of death. And all of these are man-made fears that can be mastered with a positive mental attitude.

ALDERFER:

Aren't we born with a natural capacity for fear? And isn't fear of help to us at times?

NAPOLEON HILL:

Those are very good questions, but I must call your attention to the difference between fears based upon sound reasons for their existence and fears that have no such basis whatsoever. For example, fear of the consequences of recklessness in driving an automobile is a constructive fear. But even in this case it would be much better if one expressed great faith in his ability to drive safely rather than fear. And the fear of poverty can be a healthy fear only if it serves to make one become resourceful and thrifty.

ALDERFER:

Yes, I see what you mean. Fear can become useful only by transmuting it from the negative to the positive state of mind, where it may be turned into a driving force of great benefit.

And now will you give us the fifth of the Twelve Great Riches?

NAPOLEON HILL:

Number five is the Hope of Future Achievement. The greatest of all forms of happiness comes from the hope of some as-yet-unattained desirable aim or purpose. It is this hope that has been responsible for all human progress, and it is the means by which one may keep on keeping on, with good spirits, when the going is hard and success looks far distant. Poor indeed is the person who cannot and does not look to the future with hope that he will become the person he would like to be or attain the purposes he most desires, and with the belief that he will attain those purposes.

Without hope, expressed by the signers of the Declaration of Independence, there would be no free America today. Without hope there would have been no vaccine for the mastery of polio. Without hope on the part of the faithful there would be no civilization, and we would still be living in the dark ages of cruelty and fear. Truly, hope is the salvation of the individual, the promise of a greater future for all of us.

ALDERFER:

Hope is the periscope that lets us see the clear sky above us when we are submerged by human problems, the telescope that gives us a look at the far distant star of opportunity, the road map that guides us to our destination over new and strange pathways we have not traveled before.

And now the sixth of the Twelve Great Riches.

NAPOLEON HILL:

Number six is the Capacity for Faith. Faith is the connecting link between the mind of man and the great universal reservoir of Infinite Intelligence. It is the fertile soil of the garden of the human mind, wherein one may plant the seeds of one's desires with full assurance that they will germinate and grow until they produce all of the riches one desires. Faith is the eternal elixir that gives creative power and action to the impulses of human thought. It is the basis of all miracles, and many of the mysteries that cannot be explained by ordinary logic or past experience. Faith is the power that transmutes the ordinary energies of thought into their spiritual equivalents. And it is the only means by which the cosmic forces of Infinite Intelligence may be appropriated to the uses of man.

ALDERFER:

You might have added that faith renders the word "impossible" useless and makes all things possible for the person who knows what he wants and goes after it.

And now the seventh of the Twelve Great Riches.

NAPOLEON HILL:

Number seven is a Willingness to Share One's Blessings. He who has not learned the blessed act of sharing has not found the true path to happiness, for happiness comes only by sharing. And let it be forever remembered that all riches may be embellished by the simple process of sharing them where they may serve others. Let it be remembered, also, that the space one occupies in the hearts of his fellow men is determined precisely by the services he renders through some form of sharing.

ALDERFER:

When you stop to think about it, you recognize that the supposedly wealthy person who hoards his possessions and shares them with no one is the most miserable of persons. We might observe, also, that love, the most profound of all the human emotions, is something we can enjoy only by giving it away.

This brings us to the eighth of the Twelve Great Riches.

NAPOLEON HILL:

Number eight is a Labor of Love. There can be no richer man than he who has found a labor of love and who is busily engaged in performing it, for labor is one of the highest forms of expression of human desire. Labor is the connecting link between demand and supply of all human needs, the forerunner of all human progress, the medium by which the imagination is given the wings of action. And all labor of love is sanctified because it brings the joy of self-expression, and it takes the drudgery out of all human endeavor.

ALDERFER:

I conjecture that it was a labor of love that carried you through the lean years of research while you were organizing the world's first practical philosophy of personal achievement. I have observed that when a man is engaged in doing that which he loves to do, he doesn't seem to become tired, and his endurance is beyond human comprehension, which leads to the conclusion that a labor of love has in it something closely akin to the soul of man.

Next, we have the ninth of the Twelve Great Riches.

NAPOLEON HILL:

Number nine is an Open Mind on All Subjects. Tolerance, which is among the higher attributes of culture, is expressed only by the person who holds an open mind on all subjects at all times. It is only the person with an open mind who becomes truly educated and thus prepared to avail himself of the greater blessings of life. It has been said that as long as a man remains green with an open and curious mind, he may grow bigger and wiser, but when he becomes ripe with fixed opinions and judgments, he next becomes rotten with decay.

ALDERFER:

You might well have added, also, that a man with a closed mind is generally not very well liked by others.

What is number ten of the Twelve Great Riches?

NAPOLEON HILL:

Number ten is Self-Discipline. The person who is not the master of himself may never become the master of anything else. But he who is the master of self may become the master of his own earthly destiny. And the highest form of self-discipline consists in the expression of humility of the heart after one has acquired great riches or has been met by that which is commonly called success.

ALDERFER:

Without self-discipline it is not possible for one to exercise full and complete control over his own mind, as the Creator intended that all should do. Isn't that true?

NAPOLEON HILL:

Yes, that's absolutely true, and it is one of the best reasons why one should develop the habit of self-discipline. A man without adequate discipline over his thoughts and deeds is like a ship without a rudder, and he must go wherever the waves of the ocean of life carry him.

ALDERFER:

Under what circumstances is self-discipline most essential for the person who hopes to attain outstanding success in his chosen calling?

NAPOLEON HILL:

Without hesitation I would say self-discipline is most essential in connection with one's habits of thinking, since all acts and deeds are but the expressions of thoughts. But don't forget that self-discipline is a wonderful healer of disease, a miraculous destroyer of fear and worry, and the only means by which we may take possession of our own minds and direct them to ends of our own choice, as the Creator provided we should. And it is the means by which we can give ourselves protection against those who endeavor to make us angry and thereby weaken us for their own selfish purposes.

ALDERFER:

It would seem, then, that self-discipline should have been nearer the head of the list of the Twelve Great Riches.

NAPOLEON HILL:

It would have been if the Twelve Great Riches had been presented in the order of their relative values, which is not the case. I might add that self-discipline is the means by which we may keep our mind fixed on the circumstances and things we desire most in life, and off those we do not desire.

ALDERFER:

One of the most promising benefits of self-discipline is the fact that it can be self-acquired without the permission of others. If we look around, it becomes obvious that people who are poverty-stricken, and those who are sick and ailing, and those who are in trouble with the law are generally most conspicuous by their lack of self-discipline.

NAPOLEON HILL:

That's true. Show me a person who exercises perfect discipline over self, and I'll show you a person who is a success in whatever he undertakes. He has sound health; he is happy; and he is liked by all who know him. The lack of self-restraint on the part of individuals is one, if not the main cause of the fear and chaos throughout the world today. The salvation of mankind depends upon vitally needed changes in individuals who will use enough self-discipline to get back to the fundamentals of religion and live by these instead of merely professing to believe in them. Belief is not enough. There must be deeds to back up the belief.

ALDERFER:

What you have just said about the virtues of self-discipline is so complete that you have left me no room for further comment on it, so we will pass on to the eleventh of the Twelve Great Riches.

NAPOLEON HILL:

Number eleven is the Capacity to Understand People. The person who is rich in the capacity to understand other people always recognizes that all people are fundamentally alike in that they have evolved from the same stem, and that all human activities are inspired by one or more of the same basic motives.

ALDERFER:

Under what circumstances is it most beneficial to have the capacity to understand other people?

NAPOLEON HILL:

I would say in connection with our relations with those whom we do not particularly like or with those with whom we definitely disagree. It is not difficult to understand those with whom we have no conflict of opinions, but it is a different story when we are dealing with those who disagree with us.

ALDERFER:

Does the capacity to understand other people carry with it other advantages?

NAPOLEON HILL:

Yes, it definitely enables one to become more flexible in his relations with others, and enables one to adapt himself to unpleasant circumstances without losing his temper or his composure. It also enables one to transmute hatred of others into pity and to temper his judgments of others with mercy and forgiveness when one has been injured or wronged. The capacity to understand others helps one to make allowances for their weaknesses and to give full credit for their virtues.

ALDERFER:

This brings us to the last of the Twelve Great Riches, and it happens to be the one that many people would have placed at the head of the list instead of the foot, and I know you will have some illuminating observations to make regarding the accumulation and usages of money.

NAPOLEON HILL:

Number twelve is Economic Security, or more plainly stated, Money. The reason I have not given Money first place among the Twelve Great Riches of Life stems from my observation of those who have money in great amounts but lack some or all of the other things that make people truly rich.

ALDERFER:

I notice you have not included peace of mind as one of the essentials of riches. Shouldn't this have been included in your list?

NAPOLEON HILL:

Peace of mind is, or should be, one of the greatest of all riches. I did not include it because all those who have acquired the Twelve Great Riches we have mentioned have also found peace of mind. And they have found happiness, which is the objective all people are seeking and perhaps the only major objective of life.

ALDERFER:

Will those who acquire the first eleven of the Twelve Great Riches automatically come into possession of the twelfth, which is money?

NAPOLEON HILL:

No, but these will lay the foundation for the accumulation of money. The actual acquisition of money begins by the development of a money consciousness—that is, a deep and enduring desire for money. This will naturally lead to the rendering of service or the exchange of things of value that entitle one to acquire money. Moreover, those who acquire the first eleven of the Great Riches will not only be in a position to acquire money, but more important, they will be able to use money wisely.

ALDERFER:

But, isn't it possible to acquire money in large amounts without the aid of the other eleven Great Riches?

NAPOLEON HILL:

Certainly, it is, but I implore you to observe carefully what happens to those who do so. You will discover, in every such instance, that those who acquire money in large amounts without first acquiring the other eleven Great Riches do not use the money wisely, and often it turns out that they paid too dearly for their monetary riches.

ALDERFER:

Perhaps you who are listening to this program would like to add a few items of your own that would be essential for you to acquire before you would consider yourself rich. Therefore, I suggest that you write down the entire list of the Twelve Great Riches, and then add to it those of your own choice that you deem necessary to give you absolute riches in your life.

NAPOLEON HILL:

That's an excellent idea. And I will add another suggestion to Henry's, namely, that you will find it helpful if you make a list of all of your riches, material and otherwise, and express your gratitude each night in the form of a prayer for these blessings. You will discover that the more you give thanks to the Giver of all gifts for the blessings you now possess, still other and greater blessings will be added unto you. We are living in an age of over plenty of everything except gratitude for that which we have.

ALDERFER:

And now may I make an observation regarding the Twelve Great Riches that may be of great benefit to our audience? May I call your attention to the fact that not one of the Twelve Great Riches is beyond your reach; not one of them is difficult to acquire; and they can be acquired without regard to your age, education, race, or religion. And they can be acquired without your having to ask permission of anyone for the privilege of acquiring them. Isn't this an encouraging observation?

NAPOLEON HILL:

Now that you know what makes people truly rich, what are you going to do about it? And when are you going to begin? May I suggest that the best place for you to begin is by writing out a complete list of the Twelve Great Riches and placing this list where you can check yourself against it daily for the next thirty days. Go over the list of the Great Riches one by one and place an "OK" after those you believe you have already acquired, and a zero after those that you still lack.

ALDERFER:

By this method you will soon learn to take accurate inventory of your riches, and you will develop a consciousness that will lead you to the acquisition of those that you do not already possess. Self-inventory is something we should all conduct as regularly as the successful merchant takes inventory of his merchandise.

NAPOLEON HILL:

May I suggest, also, that you have someone who knows you very well double-check your own rating on each of the Twelve Great Riches, since it is a common habit for human beings to err in their own favor when they take inventory of their blessings and their good qualities. Let your husband or wife, or some close friend who will dare to tell you the truth about yourself, have a look at your rating on the Twelve Great Riches, and you may make discoveries of great benefit to yourself.

ALDERFER:

As Napoleon Hill has so often said, "If you are ready for a thing, it will make its appearance." Paraphrasing that statement, if you are ready for the Twelve Great Riches, or any one or more of them, they will make their appearance under circumstances that you will be able to recognize and embrace. Thank you, Napoleon Hill, for your explanation of the Twelve Great Riches of Life.

Radio listeners, please tune in again next week when Napoleon Hill will discuss the "Big Four" of the success principles. The broadcast will also include a special guest who exemplifies these principles.

△

WISDOM TO LIVE BY

1. The difference between poverty and riches is not measurable in money or material possessions alone. There are Twelve Riches, eleven of which are not material, but they are closely related to the spiritual forces available to all of us.

2. Men and women who master and apply Napoleon Hill's philosophy have economic security because they possess the means by which money can be acquired. They may run out of money or lose it through poor judgment, but this does not deprive them of economic security, because they know the source of money and how to contact and benefit by that source.

3. The Twelve Great Riches of Life can bring you peace of mind and give you a well-balanced life consisting of every circumstance and every material thing you need or desire.

ADVERSITY AND ADVANTAGE

1. When we say every adversity, every unpleasant circumstance, every failure, and every physical pain carry with it the seed of an equivalent benefit, we will not be able to find that seed until we condition our mind with the Twelve Great Riches of Life explained in this chapter.

2. Suffering, disappointment, frustration, and sorrow can make us great or make us go down in permanent failure. The determining factor as to which of the two circumstances one embraces depends entirely upon one's mental attitude toward them.

3. Failure is a blessing or a curse, depending upon the individual's reaction to it. If one looks upon failure as a sort of nudge from the hand of destiny, which signals one to move in another direction, and if one acts on that signal, the experience is practically sure to become a blessing. If one accepts failure as an indication of one's weakness and broods over it until it produces an inferiority complex, then it is a curse. The nature of the reaction tells the story, and this is under the exclusive control of the individual at all times.

▼

CHAPTER 11

THE BIG FOUR

(A TICKET TO FAVORABLE BREAKS)

△

"The man or woman who does not give fair service for which
he or she is paid is dishonest, and one who is not willing to give
more than this is foolish."

Charles Schwab

OVERVIEW

In this chapter, Hill revisits the concept of Going the Extra Mile he introduced in Chapter 2. The purpose of this lesson is to reinforce the wisdom that no one has ever achieved outstanding success without practicing the habit of Going the Extra Mile.

Hill will explain how:

- Knowing and understanding the concept of Going the Extra Mile will not only give you favorable breaks but also start to produce miracles in your life

- Experiencing the results of this habit will inspire you to greater efforts and will never make you feel disappointed or discouraged

Applying the principle of Going the Extra Mile is of such importance that without it one cannot become a true success. Once you understand the power of applying this principle without fail throughout your life, you will have the ability to succeed where others have not.

BROADCAST 11. THE BIG FOUR

ANNOUNCER:

Good afternoon, ladies and gentlemen. The Radio School of the Air is on the air. Napoleon Hill's famed philosophy of success is being presented to you in these radio lessons. Napoleon Hill has a long and successful background. Time just won't allow me to go into it at length. Today's lesson features a guest who followed the principles of success developed and proved by Napoleon Hill. Assisting Mr. Hill is Henry Alderfer, associate director of education of the Success School of the Air. And now, here is Mr. Alderfer.

ALDERFER:

Thank you. Well, friends, we have a surprise for you today. We have been telling you on these Sunday programs how people attain success, and today we have as our guest a man who has made himself very successful here in Chicago. Like most people who rise to great heights of success, our guest started at the bottom, and he made a place for himself by following the very same success principles we have been presenting on this program. Here is Napoleon Hill, who will tell you why this particular man was chosen as our guest, and he will pinpoint for you the particular success principles that were used by him. And now, Napoleon Hill.

NAPOLEON HILL:

Good afternoon, my friends. Before we introduce our guest I wish to remind you that no one ever rises to noteworthy heights of success without applying the Big Four success principles. These are Definiteness of Purpose, the Master Mind, Applied Faith, and the habit of Going the Extra Mile. You'll observe that our guest not only made use of the Big Four success principles, but he also used other success principles that you'll be able to recognize.

ALDERFER:

Yes, he definitely made use of the principles of a Pleasing Personality, Enthusiasm, Profiting by Adversity, Concentration of Effort, and a Positive Mental Attitude, as you will observe when you hear his story. However, one of the success principles stood out above all the others in his relations with other people.

NAPOLEON HILL:

Of course, you have reference to the habit of Going the Extra Mile. It is very obvious that our guest not only goes out of his way to render more service than he is paid for, but he actually does so because he likes people and desires to see everyone get ahead.

ALDERFER:

Our guest is Mel Thillens, president of a check-cashing company in which he operates a fleet of armored trucks that cash paychecks for the employees of some 1,200 firms in the Chicago area, serving both day and night shifts twenty-four hours per day. Mel is a fine example of a successful businessman who believes in sharing his success with others. After having met with reverses that would have discouraged the average man from aiming at success anywhere near to the upper brackets of achievement, Mel Thillens began his unique check-cashing business with $300 of borrowed capital, which he managed so effectively that his firm now cashes upward of seven million dollars of paychecks every week. And now, Napoleon Hill will take over and help Mel to give you his dramatic story, which clearly shows that every adversity carries with it the seed of an equivalent advantage.

NAPOLEON HILL:

Welcome to our program, Mel Thillens. We are happy to have you here because you are a living example of a man who has attained outstanding success using principles we have been presenting on this program. And now, Mel, I want you please to briefly describe every job you held before you got into business for yourself. What was your first job, and when did you have it?

THILLENS:

My first job was with a Chicago bank at the age of sixteen. That was back at the beginning of the business Depression. The bank closed because of the Depression, and I was out of a job, but I was not out of hope, for I knew that somewhere I would find a place right for me.

NAPOLEON HILL:

In other words, when the going was hard for you, instead of giving up and quitting, you turned on more steam and made up your mind that in a great country like ours, there is no legitimate reason for anyone to give up hope. What was your next move?

THILLENS:

One of the executives of the closed bank went into business for himself. He opened a currency exchange and he gave me a job with his new enterprise.

He had observed my willingness to render service beyond that which was expected of me, and that probably was one reason why he employed me.

NAPOLEON HILL:

Well, Mel, how did your new job turn out?

THILLENS:

It didn't turn out so well. In fact, it turned me out and folded up in a short while because business conditions were so bad that it began to lose money heavily.

NAPOLEON HILL:

Well, old Lady Luck was sure giving you a runaround, and I suppose the loss of two jobs in rapid succession was pretty discouraging, wasn't it?

THILLENS:

No, I was disappointed but not discouraged, for I knew that the sort of service I was willing to render would pay off somewhere, somehow. The bank executive who opened the currency exchange moved out of the office we occupied, but I didn't move. I stayed on and kept books, without pay, for a real estate firm that occupied the same office.

NAPOLEON HILL:

You were going the extra mile, even when adversity had overtaken you, and that was the very place where the average person gives up and quits or expects someone to give him a lift. You were undergoing a severe testing time, and that was a wonderful experience because it introduced you to your Other Self—that self that converts stumbling blocks into stepping-stones to opportunity. What was your next move?

THILLENS:

I reached a decision that required lots of nerve, but it proved to have been the right direction. I decided to reopen the currency exchange. I had no capital, but I got a loan of $300 from a small loan company and opened up. I continued to keep books for the real estate firm in the same office in return for the use of the space I occupied.

NAPOLEON HILL:

I suppose the sailing was easy for you from there on, and your troubles were over.

THILLENS:

As far as troubles were concerned, I have never recognized any adverse circumstance as trouble but only as an inspiration for greater effort. And you can well imagine that the small $300 operating capital I had, when I actually needed much more, gave me plenty to think about before I got over the hump, into what you call "easy sailing."

NAPOLEON HILL:

Mel, just how did you manage to operate a check-cashing business on capital of only $300 and also make a living from so small an amount of operating capital?

THILLENS:

If a man's success plan is sound and he has confidence in himself, he will always find a way to carry out his plans. I made the $300 of working capital serve for the time being by "doubling in brass," you might say. Specifically, I kept my working capital available in the cash drawer by rushing over to the bank and cashing checks as fast as I took them in. True, I wore out a lot of shoe leather in this way, but I did not wear out my patience or my faith. Also, I soon hit upon another plan that gave me a favorable break. I discovered that some of my best customers had enough confidence in me to leave their paychecks with me in return for a receipt, and this gave me a chance to go to the bank and cash the checks before I handed the money over to the customers, sometimes a day or so later.

NAPOLEON HILL:

I suppose you got some other favorable breaks along the way. People who have faith in themselves and are willing to go the extra mile always attract favorable breaks somehow.

THILLENS:

Yes, I got a favorable break, you might say, when the workers on a government construction job in my neighborhood began to cash their checks in my exchange. But this break also had some headaches in it, because the long lines of construction employees that crowded into my place on payday disrupted my regular business so completely that I knew I had to do something about it.

NAPOLEON HILL:

Once more you were at a turning point where you had to reach a decision that probably called for both courage and a financial risk. Also, once more you were faced by an opportunity to learn what sort of stuff Mel Thillens was made of. What did you do about it?

THILLENS:

I decided that instead of having the construction workers line up in front of my office on payday I would cash their checks for them on the job. In order to do this, I had to have an armored truck and armed guards to protect it. I borrowed the money with which to buy the truck, and very soon my problem was converted into a thriving business. Instead of depending upon people to come to me to cash their paychecks, I decided to go to them on the job where they worked. We now serve the employees of over 1,200 Chicago firms, by cashing their paychecks without loss of time to the employees or the employer and without cost to management.

NAPOLEON HILL:

After you put into operation a fleet of armored trucks to handle your check-cashing business and you lifted the business out of the red into the black, you began to look for some means of expressing your gratitude for your success. You didn't have to look very far. About five years ago you turned your attention, and a good share of the profits of your business, to work toward the solution to the problem of juvenile delinquency in Chicago. You founded the Thillens Boys' Major Baseball League, which you are operating in your beautiful outdoor stadium on Chicago's North Side, which accepts all boys of ages from nine to twelve. Mel, will you tell us something about what you are accomplishing in the lives of these boys?

THILLENS:

For the past five years, five hundred boys each year, playing on thirty different teams, have competed in the Thillens leagues. Three games are played every night of the week throughout the summer. The games are open to the public, and admission is free. The boys are equipped with big league–type uniforms, and they play under the lights, just like their big league idols.

Besides learning the fundamentals of the game, the boys are taught clean sportsmanship and gentlemanly conduct by schooled instructors in the field of physical education. We believe our program is a great weapon in the fight against juvenile delinquency. The family is brought closer together when son, sister, dad, and mother all participate in the sport of the boys. It would do your heart good to see those boys in action, for you would know that both their minds and their bodies are being disciplined to meet the responsibilities of life they will face in later years. And they are so proud of those new uniforms that I wonder if they don't sleep in them at times!

NAPOLEON HILL:

I think this is about the finest thing I have ever heard of a businessman doing to improve the lives of boys, and I want to congratulate you, Mel, and at the same time I wish to express the hope that your example will inspire other men to give more attention to the youth of today who will become the leaders of government and business of tomorrow. I know now why you always seem so happy and also why you are so successful in your business. You not only go the extra mile in everything you do, but you actually have a lot of fun doing so, and this is my idea of making life pay off in terms of happiness as well as in material possessions.

THILLENS:

It may interest you to know, Mr. Hill, that our business began to thrive in a really big way in almost exact proportion to the effort we spent in developing the Thillens Boys' Major Baseball League. Also, the happiness we have inspired in the lives of these boys has come back to us like bread cast upon the waters, to give joy and harmony and a spirit of cooperation in our business family. Many of the boys who got their start playing baseball with us now occupy responsible positions in commerce and industry and are our best goodwill ambassadors.

NAPOLEON HILL:

I have been in your office, and the first thing I observed when I walked into the building was the spirit of harmony that prevails there. I was impressed also by the fact that you refer to your business family as your associates, not as your employees, and I couldn't help wondering why the example you have established in dealing with your business associates does not prevail in all well-managed business institutions. You'll never have any labor troubles as long as you relate yourself to your associate workers so that they have a deep and abiding affection for you, as they do now.

THILLENS:

Well, Mr. Hill, I have never discovered a better way of finding happiness than that of helping others to find it, and the same goes for financial success—the best and surest way of finding it is by helping others to succeed.

NAPOLEON HILL:

Mel, I am discovering that you are not only a successful businessman, but you are a sound philosopher as well, and if you ever take a notion to give up the check-cashing business let me know, because I might add you to my team in helping other people to help themselves through positive thinking.

THILLENS:

Thank you very much, but instead of my giving up the check-cashing business you may be surprised to hear that I have hopes of making it nationwide.

NAPOLEON HILL:

And what about the Thillens Boys' Major Baseball League? Will that go along with your expansion plan of the check-cashing business, too?

THILLENS:

To be candid with you, Mr. Hill, some of my friends believe that my first love is the Boys' Major Baseball League, and I'm not denying that they are correct. I want you to come over and see our boys in action, then you will understand the reason for my affection for them. Making money is pleasant, and of course it is necessary, but making young lads into fine, upright citizens gives one a thrill that can hardly be described in words alone. Every time I read in the newspapers about some youth who has gotten into trouble with the law I cannot help believing that if he had been on one of our Boys' Major Baseball League teams he would have been safe and free from trouble.

NAPOLEON HILL:

What are your requirements for your associates, Mel?

THILLENS:

First of all, we want men with a keen sense of loyalty. Then we desire that they be dependable. Next we want them to like people and to be friendly and dress neatly. And of course, we want men who can interview business executives on their own level. And last, but perhaps most important, we want men who sincerely like to render more service and better service than that which is expected of them, for we have learned from experience that this is the type of person who makes friends for himself and our company.

NAPOLEON HILL:

Thank you, Mel Thillens, and may your every endeavor be blessed with the success you so richly deserve. And now, Henry Alderfer, I notice that you are still with us, although Mel and I have been doing most of the talking.

ALDERFER:

To be perfectly truthful, I have been so intensely interested in what you have been talking about that I hoped you would just let me listen. Isn't it a real pleasure, in this age of speed and greed, to find a man like Mel Thillens, who devotes both his time and his money to helping make better citizens of young Americans? While Mel was talking I couldn't help thinking what a miracle would take place in the city of Chicago if only a hundred successful businessmen should set aside a portion of their time and their money to help both boys and girls to find themselves through clean sports properly supervised by competent directors. If we could multiply Mel Thillens by one hundred and put his humanitarian plans to work on all levels of society, there soon would be no juvenile delinquency problems in Chicago.

NAPOLEON HILL:

Yes, and I might remark that this method of going the extra mile would be just as beneficial to the sponsors as it would be to the youngsters whom they would help to get started in life on the right path. There is some strange power attached to this principle of Going the Extra Mile that often produces miracles in the lives of those who practice it. For it is true that whatever you do to or for another you do to or for yourself.

ALDERFER:

Didn't Ralph Waldo Emerson come pretty close to describing this strange power associated with the habit of Going the Extra Mile in his essay *Compensation*?

NAPOLEON HILL:

Yes, he did! And he made it quite clear that this power is not man-made but a part of that great universal system that gives us orderliness throughout the cosmic spaces of the universe. I have observed that the next best thing to that of rendering useful service is to turn the spotlight on others who are being helpful, and in this way extend their usefulness. We already have too many people engaged in uncovering the weaknesses and wrongdoings of people. May it not be desirable to ferret out the ones who are doing good in the world and set them up as examples for others to follow?

ALDERFER:

Here is an appropriate place for me to suggest that Napoleon Hill follow his own counsel by letting you, the radio listeners, take a look over his shoulder, so to speak, at a personal code of ethics he wrote for himself, entitled *Gratitude*. I think you will be interested in knowing that he wrote the code as the result of the inspiration he got from meeting and talking with Mel Thillens, which only goes to prove once again that you cannot rub elbows with anyone, whether they are good or bad, without some of their character rubbing off on you.

NAPOLEON HILL:

Correct, Henry, and I am going to dedicate this code of ethics to Mel Thillens. The title of the code is GRATITUDE.

GRATITUDE!

Through the bountiful hand of Destiny I have received many blessings for which I offer a deep and enduring feeling of gratitude.

I am grateful for the adversities and defeats I have experienced, for they have given me strength through struggle.

I am grateful for having experienced poverty, for it has taught me how to properly evaluate riches.

I am grateful for the misguided people who have endeavored to relate themselves to me unjustly, for they have provided me with an opportunity to forgive them.

I am grateful for the land of my birth, for it has provided me with all the opportunity for self-advancement that I can embrace and use.

I am grateful for the errors and mistakes I have made, for they have taught me the virtues of caution and accurate thinking.

I am grateful for the work to which I have dedicated my life, for it has given me the privilege of inspiring and aiding countless millions of people.

I am grateful for having had a few enemies, for they have forced me to carefully inspect myself from within and to make some needed refinements of character.

I am grateful to be able to testify that my faith is greater than all fears, and my soul is free from hatred and envy.

I am grateful for my controlled capacity for righteous indignation, for it encourages me to stand up and be counted on behalf of justice.

I am grateful for having learned the art of self-immunization against the influence of negative thoughts and deeds.

I am grateful for having witnessed the glory of the Creator through the bountiful achievements of man during the first half of the twentieth century.

And I am most profoundly grateful for having had revealed to me the doorway through which I may contact and draw upon the power of Infinite Intelligence for my every need.

Lastly, if I could have granted to me but one wish, it would be that I could share all of these blessings with my fellow men, now and always.

ALDERFER:

Thank you warmly, Napoleon Hill. And thank you, Mel Thillens, for sharing your inspiring story with our radio audience. Friends, please join us next Sunday for another broadcast, when Mr. Hill will tell you how to attain a Positive Mental Attitude.

△

WISDOM TO LIVE BY

1. Going the Extra Mile is the habit of rendering more and better service than that which one is paid for, and giving that service with a positive mental attitude. This is definitely a rule through which a person may literally write his or her own price tag and be sure of getting it.

2. You can be an encyclopedia of knowledge and still be a failure. Your intellect or education will not do you much good if you cannot get people to cooperate with you. Going the Extra Mile is the only way this can happen.

3. Any system, any philosophy, or any practice that deprives a person of the privilege of Going the Extra Mile is unsound and doomed to failure.

4. There are numerous extraordinary benefits that one can enjoy by Going the Extra Mile. It:

   a. Eliminates competition

   b. Generates continuous demand for your service

   c. Creates favorable breaks for you

   d. Generates economic security and luxuries available only to those who go the extra mile

   e. Makes you indispensable in relationships and in the workplace

   f. Leads to development of a positive, pleasing attitude and personality

g. Gives you greater confidence in yourself and puts you on a better basis with your own conscience

h. Allows you to live a life that others are blindly seeking to live up to

i. Creates opportunities

5. Your success in life is in direct proportion to what you do after you do what you are expected to do. And that little extra may be all that you need to succeed.

ADVERSITY AND ADVANTAGE

1. Adversity comes to those who consistently shirk their work and think that they are justified in trying to deceive their employer on the grounds that they are underpaid. Such people are not only unfit to rise out of their poverty but are actually putting themselves into a deeper hole of misery and poverty.

2. The only way out of this misery is to start practicing the habit of Going the Extra Mile. Since the majority of people do not practice Going the Extra Mile, you have a tremendous opportunity, greater than ever before, to succeed if you will act on, adopt, and follow this master strategy.

▼

CHAPTER 12

FACTORS OF A POSITIVE MENTAL ATTITUDE

(A PRICELESS ASSET)

"People who control their mental attitudes
control their destinies."

Napoleon Hill

OVERVIEW

Hill explains the principle of a Positive Mental Attitude in chapter 9. However, here he teaches us how to maintain this attitude at all times and make it a habit that:

- Turns every experience, whether it is pleasant or unpleasant, to some benefit that leads to peace of mind

- Helps you search for "the seed of equivalent benefit" that comes with every failure, adversity, or defeat

- Evaluates all problems that can be solved and those you cannot control

- Keeps your mind on the things you want and off the things you don't desire

- Helps you march forward toward the attainment of your definite purpose without hesitation

- Conditions your mind to eliminate all kinds of fears

Hill's lesson will show you how Positive Mental Attitude is a priceless asset that, when used to its full extent, ensures you will never sway from your goals.

BROADCAST 12. FACTORS OF A POSITIVE MENTAL ATTITUDE

ANNOUNCER:
Good afternoon, ladies and gentlemen. The Radio School of Success Unlimited is on the air. Napoleon Hill's famed philosophy of success is being presented to you in these thirteen lessons. Napoleon Hill has a long and successful background. Time just won't allow me to go into it at length, but today's lesson, which you will hear in a moment, follows the principles of success developed and proved by Napoleon Hill. Assisting Mr. Hill is

Mr. Henry Alderfer, associate director of education of the Napoleon Hill Institute. Now here is Mr. Alderfer.

ALDERFER:

Thank you. We've another treat for you this afternoon. Napoleon Hill told you in a previous broadcast that a positive mental attitude is number one of the Twelve Great Riches of Life. Now he'll break down this subject and describe for you one by one the factors that will gain for you a positive mental attitude. There's always a starting point from which one must take off in this pursuit of success, and he will tell you where to begin in forming the habit of a positive mental attitude. And here is Napoleon Hill.

NAPOLEON HILL:

Good afternoon, my radio friends. Well, first of all, to develop the habit of a positive mental attitude, you must learn to adjust yourself to other people's state of mind and to their peculiarities so as to get along peacefully with them even though you may not always agree with them. And above all you must refrain from emphasizing trivial circumstances in your relationships with others by refusing to allow them to become controversial incidents.

ALDERFER:

For example, if I do something you don't like or say something that displeases you, it's best to keep quiet rather than to start an argument. Is that the gist of what you just said?

NAPOLEON HILL:

Yes, but that's only a part of the answer. You might have added that the person who keeps his mind positive not only refuses to engage in small talk or unimportant arguments, but he deliberately and diplomatically switches the conversation to subjects of his own choosing in order to keep out of unnecessary arguments.

ALDERFER:

Isn't this how the master salesman relates himself to an argumentative buyer?

NAPOLEON HILL:

Yes, and let's remember that all of us are salesmen, or we should be, in that it is our responsibility to learn how to relate ourselves to other people so as to avoid antagonizing them. Also, let us remember that the master salesman knows that the most important person living is the one to whom he's trying to make a sale, and he makes it his business to condition the mind of the buyer by keeping the conversation directed to subjects on which he and the buyer are apt to agree.

ALDERFER:

What about the salesman's own mental attitude? Can he make sales when his mind is negative?

NAPOLEON HILL:

No, because a negative mental attitude is contagious, and it's picked up by a prospective buyer and passed right back to the salesman in the form of a no.

ALDERFER:

It seems necessary then to develop a definite technique or system for keeping the mind positive at all times when we're dealing with others. Do you know of such a system that's practical?

NAPOLEON HILL:

Well, yes, there are many systems, but the greatest master salesman I have ever known makes it his business never to enter into any human relationship or any form of negotiation with others without having first expressed his silent prayer that every word he may express will be adorned by a spirit of affection for those with whom he negotiates. And he closes his prayer by an expression of gratitude for having met with success in his negotiation even before he begins to negotiate. Search wherever you will, but you'll never find a more effective method than this for conditioning the mind to remain positive.

ALDERFER:

What are some of the other means of conditioning the mind to become positive?

NAPOLEON HILL:

Perhaps I can best answer this question by giving you in my own words my own system, which has served me so effectively that I have been privileged to render useful service to men and women throughout the world. Here it is. Every night before I retire I express a prayer of gratitude for all of the blessings I have received in the past and all I hope to receive in the future. Here it is. Oh Divine Providence, all I hope to become I owe to the influence of other people; therefore, may I never engage in any acts or speak any words except those that encourage and enrich the minds of those with whom I deal. I am grateful for the hope, faith, and courage that have carried me over the adversities of the past. I am grateful for the spirit of benevolence I feel toward my fellow men under all circumstances. I am grateful for the spirit of compassion and forgiveness that I express for those who may offend me. I am grateful for the endurance of both body and mind, with which I meet the struggles I must face. I am grateful for the spirit of persistence, with which I am privileged to discipline my thoughts and deeds at all times. I am grateful for sound health, physically and mentally. I am grateful for having learned how to change adversity into an advantage without violating the rights of others, and I am most profoundly grateful for having mastered fear by having learned the art of transmuting it into courage and understanding. Tomorrow may I inspire all with whom I meet to embrace and express this same positive mental attitude in all of their human relations. Amen.

ALDERFER:

Wonderful. Isn't it difficult to maintain a positive mental attitude when other people intrude upon your rights and sorely try your patience?

NAPOLEON HILL:

No one can make you angry without your full consent and your cooperation. No one can change your mental attitude in any respect whatsoever without your consent. Your mental attitude can be always of your own choice because you have complete control over your own mind.

ALDERFER:

What's the next step that one uses in forming the habit of a positive mental attitude?

NAPOLEON HILL:

It's a mighty good practice to form the habit of having a good hearty laugh when you are tempted to become angry. But be sure to get out of sight of others when you do this so you'll not be ridiculed. Laughing changes the chemistry of the mind from negative to positive. This is worth remembering, no matter who you are or what may be your calling. I know a man now well along in his nineties who attributes his longevity to his strict habit of laughing heartily every day. It may sound insignificant, but just try it! Laughing will make a big difference in your attitude.

ALDERFER:

What's the next step that you'd recommend for those who wish to keep a positive mental attitude at all times?

NAPOLEON HILL:

Form the habit of concentrating your mind upon the "can do" in connection with all of your problems and objectives. Remember there is always some move you can make that will be helpful, no matter what your problem may be. Take that move, and you will discover that it leads to another and still other moves you can make until you attain success. Most people concentrate their minds on the "cannot do" part of their plans and problems. That is, they think of all of the obstacles that may get in their way, and they have no time left for that "can do" start that they could make.

ALDERFER:

Isn't it true that the conditions of modern civilization are such that everyone must meet with a certain amount of unpleasant circumstances as they move along in the daily business of living? How can one maintain a positive mental attitude when everything goes wrong, when there's not enough money to pay debts, when sickness creeps into the family, business depressions come along, wars are thrust upon us, and trusted friends prove to be untrustworthy? Don't these circumstances make it difficult for one to keep his mind positive?

NAPOLEON HILL:

Henry, everything that's worth having has a price one must pay, and it has been so arranged by an all-wise Creator that our strength grows out of our struggles. Just remember that every circumstance that influences your life, either pleasantly or unpleasantly, is a lesson for your life, and you can use it to your advantage by relating yourself to it with a positive mental attitude.

ALDERFER:

What's the next step in maintaining a positive mental attitude?

NAPOLEON HILL:

I tend to look upon life as a continuous process of learning from experience, both the good and the bad, so I am always on the alert for gains of wisdom that come a little at a time, day by day, from both the pleasant and the unpleasant experiences. Just remember as you go along that no one can be 100 percent successful in all of his aims and purposes, and learn that failures and defeats oftentimes turn out to be blessings in disguise. Especially is this so when they turn one away from doing something that would've turned out disastrously to oneself or to others.

ALDERFER:

We might profit by remembering that more than 1900 years ago a very wise prophet came among us whose sole mission was that of teaching us how to help ourselves by helping others. But despite the soundness of his teachings, he did not get 100 percent acceptance of them. So who are we to imagine that we can go through life without experiencing some failures and defeat?

What's the next step in the maintenance of a positive mental attitude?

NAPOLEON HILL:

Make this world over by all means if you don't like it as it is, but begin with yourself in some form of self-improvement that will set a good example for others to emulate. There's never been any greater method of teaching others to live correctly than that of following the habit of living correctly ourselves.

ALDERFER:

Now will you tell us how we may change an unpleasant experience into a definite benefit by positive thinking?

NAPOLEON HILL:

The best example I can think of is that of the fear of criticism. Perhaps this fear retards the progress of people more often than any other, and this despite the fact that constructive criticism can become of great benefit if one accepts it as such. The way to benefit by criticism is to accept it as an occasion for self-examination to determine how much of it is justified. One may make startling discoveries about himself because of criticism if he accepts it solely as an inspiration to unbiased self-examination and not as an occasion for resentment.

ALDERFER:

Shouldn't one differentiate between friendly and unfriendly criticism?

NAPOLEON HILL:

No, the major advantage that one may get from criticism is that it can inspire self-analysis. If the criticism is justified, it gives one an opportunity to improve himself by removing the cause. If it is not justified it gives one an opportunity to reinforce his confidence in himself and his own judgment.

It may be human to resent criticism, but it is wisdom to learn to profit by it whether we like it or not. I don't suppose that anyone ever learns to actually like to be criticized, but one can still benefit from it.

ALDERFER:

Now comes the sixty-four-dollar question. What are the most outstanding benefits one may receive from following the habit of having a positive mental attitude?

NAPOLEON HILL:

Well, first of all, let me give you this daily creed of a man who has learned how to maintain a positive mental attitude. The title of it is *A Happy Man's Creed*, and here it is. I have found happiness by helping others to find it. I have sound physical health because I live temperately in all things and keep my mind attuned to a positive mental attitude. I am free from fear in all of its forms. I hate no man, envy no man, but love all mankind. I am engaged in a labor of love with which I mix play generously; therefore, I never grow tired. I give thanks daily not for more riches but for more wisdom with which to recognize and to properly use the great abundance of riches I now have at my command. I speak no name save only to honor it. I ask no favors except the privilege of sharing my blessings with all who are ready to receive them. I am on good terms with my own conscience. I am free from greed and covet only the material things I can use while I live, and my greatest wish is that all mankind may learn to accept life and to use it as I am doing.

ALDERFER:

That's a wonderful creed to live by, and the best part of it consists in the fact that anyone who desires to may adopt it and use it. What are some of the other benefits of adopting a positive mental attitude?

NAPOLEON HILL:

A positive mental attitude gives one complete mastery over self. It gives one freedom from want. It aids in freeing one from physical and mental ailments. It gives one freedom from the superstitions of the past that have held mankind in bondage through the years. It frees one from the common habit of seeking something for nothing. It aids one in thinking accurately on all subjects, and it inspires frequent self-inspection from within, which leads to the refinement of character.

ALDERFER:

It would seem that the benefits you've mentioned would more than justify the time and the effort that's required to develop the habit of a positive mental attitude.

NAPOLEON HILL:

Yes, it does, but I'm not through yet. A positive mental attitude gives one the necessary courage to look for the facts of life as a realist and not as an impractical dreamer. It discourages greed and the desire to become great and powerful at the expense of others. It inspires one to help others to help themselves.

ALDERFER:

Surely, you've mentioned about all of the benefits one may get from the habit of a positive mental attitude, haven't you?

NAPOLEON HILL:

No, I've only just begun. A positive mental attitude helps one to recognize that no one has exclusive privileges in the approach to the powers of Infinite Intelligence. And it gives one freedom from fear and anxiety over what may happen after that change that we call death. It inspires one to follow the habit of Going the Extra Mile by rendering more service and better service than that which is expected of him. It gives one freedom from discouragement even in the face of the most trying circumstances. It inspires one to think in terms of that which one desires to do and not of the obstacles one may have to overcome in doing it.

ALDERFER:

It seems there's no end to the benefits one may enjoy through positive thinking. Are there still more to come?

NAPOLEON HILL:

Oh yes, much more than time will permit me to mention, but here are some of the more important benefits. A positive mental attitude inspires one to look for the seed of an equivalent advantage in every adversity and every failure. It inspires one to take life in stride, neither shrinking from the disagreeable, nor overindulging in the pleasantries of life. It aids one in making life pay off on one's own terms rather than settling for a menial job. It helps one to evaluate poverty as something one doesn't have to accept as anything more than an inspiration to greater effort.

ALDERFER:

I'm happy to report to you that the mail we are receiving from the listeners to this program clearly expresses the same profound hopes for a better world such as Mr. Hill has described on this and previous programs. The world is hungry for freedom from fear, and the people are ready and willing to follow the leadership of someone who offers a practical means of freedom from fear.

NAPOLEON HILL:

This leadership must become activated in business and industry and the professions and in politics and in religion, where a relatively few people influence and guide the destinies of the masses who depend upon them for sound guidance. Wherever there is a great need, there is also a great opportunity.

ALDERFER:

Thank you, Napoleon Hill. Listeners, please join us next Sunday for our final broadcast in this series, in which Mr. Hill will review the principles he has presented so well in previous weeks.

WISDOM TO LIVE BY

The importance of having a **positive mental attitude:**

1. Mental attitude is the one and only thing over which anyone has been given the complete, unchallengeable privilege of personal control.

2. Your mental attitude determines, to a large extent, whether you find peace of mind or go through life in a state of frustration and misery.

3. Your mental attitude is the major factor that attracts people to you in a spirit of friendliness or repels them, according to whether your attitude is positive or negative; you are the only person who can determine which it shall be.

4. Your mental attitude is the only condition of mind in which you can meet and recognize your Other Self, the self that knows no self-limitations. It is that self that always remains in possession of your mind and directs it to a predetermined desired end and to the solution of each problem.

5. Mental attitude is a determining factor as to what results one gets from prayer. Only the prayers that are backed by a mental attitude of profound faith can be expected to bring positive results.

ADVERSITY AND ADVANTAGE

1. Why do some people always seem to succeed, while others always seem to fail? Perhaps the answer lies in their basic attitude toward life and how that attitude influences how they deal with problems and opportunities. Positive minds constantly work to create positive self-esteem and results. Negative minds maintain and create negative self-esteem results.

2. Think of it this way: defeat is life's way of building our character and our resiliency. We become stronger when we face defeat. Always look for the equivalent benefit; it is always there. Embrace this seed of equivalent benefit, then move on to whatever you consider success.

3. If you accept defeat as an inspiration to try again with renewed confidence and determination, attaining success will be only a matter of time. The secret to this is your positive mental attitude.

▼

CHAPTER 13

THE GOLDEN RULE

(BRINGING YOU PEACE OF MIND)

△

*"There is no defeat except from within. There is
really no insurmountable barrier, except your own
inherent weakness of purpose."*

Emerson

OVERVIEW

This final chapter will enable you to use profitably and constructively all of the knowledge acquired in the preceding lessons.

Hill discusses:

- Why only 2 percent of people know what they want and believe they are going to get it

- One trait that, when you acquire it, will help you grow and become stronger

- One power within you that makes failure impossible

- One habit that helps you rise above mediocrity

- The one and only universal rule, which, if applied for personal and professional success, will give you peace of mind

Together with the preceding twelve chapters, this lesson will reinforce all the concepts, principles, and strategies for overcoming adversity and achieving peace of mind. Embrace these learnings with consistency and passion and you will have all of what you need to obtain your goals and succeed in your dreams.

BROADCAST 13. REVIEW

ALDERFER:

Good afternoon, radio friends. This is our final broadcast in this Chicago radio series. For the benefit of those who may not have heard the first of our programs we are going to review some of the more important of the success principles that we covered in our earlier presentations.

Now here is Napoleon Hill, who will first describe for you what may be the most important of all the success principles. It is important because it is the starting point of all successful achievements. Napoleon Hill.

NAPOLEON HILL:

The starting point of all successful achievements is Definiteness of Purpose, that is, knowing precisely what you want, how much of it you want, and when you desire to get it.

ALDERFER:

This seems like a very simple success principle, one that every person can follow very easily.

NAPOLEON HILL:

Yes, it is a simple principle, but not everyone understands its importance. You may be surprised to learn that only two out of every hundred people know what they want in life, and these are the ones who are successful. They are our leaders in business and industry and the professions.

ALDERFER:

Do these two out of every hundred people, who are successful because they know what they want, have more ability or more education than the ninety-eight who do not know what they want? Or just what is it that helps them to succeed where the others fail?

NAPOLEON HILL:

No, they do not have more education necessarily, and they have no more potential ability than the failures. They simply know what they want, and they attune their mental attitude to attain this goal. At this point they tune in and contact an invisible power that helps them to overcome all obstacles.

ALDERFER:

Is there another success principle that helps the successful people to overcome the obstacles that get in their way?

NAPOLEON HILL:

Yes, people who know what they want and are determined to settle with life for nothing less automatically recognize and embrace another powerful success principle known as Applied Faith. With the aid of Applied Faith the successful people not only know what they want but they believe in their ability to get it, believe so strongly, that they can see themselves in possession of whatever they desire, even before they start after it.

ALDERFER:

In other words, the person who makes use of Applied Faith does not sell himself short, but believes in that world-famous saying, whatever the mind can conceive and believe, the mind can achieve.

NAPOLEON HILL:

That is the idea precisely. When Thomas Edison began his investigation in search of the means of creating a light with electricity, he made use of the two most powerful of the success principles. He knew what he wanted, and he believed he would find it, although his faith was severely tested through thousands of failures.

ALDERFER:

Isn't it true that our faith is tested often until we reach the point where it is so strong that it needs no additional testing? And isn't it true that most people give up and quit when their faith is undergoing this testing time?

NAPOLEON HILL:

Yes, unfortunately most people fail to pass the testing of their faith, but those who do pass the testing successfully are the leaders in every calling on earth. They are the builders of business and industry and the strong arm of civilization itself.

ALDERFER:

What is it that sustains a person in the hour of defeat, when everything seems to be going against him? When logic and reason and past experiences tell him clearly he cannot win?

NAPOLEON HILL:

I can only answer that question by calling attention to the fact that our entire lives, from birth until death, are filled with problems that call for struggle, and struggle makes for strength and growth. The Creator never gives one problems without the means of meeting and mastering them. To answer your question directly, Applied Faith is the miraculous power that sustains us in the hour of defeat and permits us to turn adversity into advantage.

ALDERFER:

In other words, the Creator gave us problems to be solved in order that we may grow strong through our struggles in solving them, and He gave us the capacity for faith so we may be strong enough to survive and become the master of our struggles. If—

NAPOLEON HILL:

Yes—if—we take possession of our own minds and direct them to ends of our own choice. We must recognize this one big *if*, and we must do something about it. Fortunately, the initiative has been left with each of us, and with this privilege goes also the responsibility of exercising it. If we meet the challenge successfully and exercise the privilege of initiative in directing our minds to ends of our own choice, we discover that there are no limitations to what we may do except those that we set up in our own minds.

ALDERFER:

Isn't it pretty difficult to convince a person who has failed that he could have succeeded with much less effort than he devoted to his failure, if only he had moved with a positive mental attitude based on Applied Faith?

NAPOLEON HILL:

Yes, one of the strangest traits of human beings is the fact that they look everywhere except in the right place for the cause of their failures, and everywhere except in the right place for the power that would make failure impossible, and that is the power of their own minds.

ALDERFER:

How may one go about recognizing and using the power of Applied Faith? There must be some success principle involved that we should describe.

NAPOLEON HILL:

Yes, there is a very important success principle that, if it is understood and followed, will lead one to the discovery of the power of Applied Faith. This principle is the habit of Going the Extra Mile, which means the rendering of more service and better service than that which is expected of us, and doing it in a positive, pleasing mental attitude.

ALDERFER:

Don't most people believe they are already doing more than they are paid for?

NAPOLEON HILL:

Yes, perhaps most people do, and may I direct your attention to the significant fact that most people are not successful? It is a well-established fact that no one ever rises above mediocrity without following the habit of Going the Extra Mile, and doing it all the time, not just now and then.

ALDERFER:

Aren't there some organizations that discourage the habit of Going the Extra Mile? In fact, don't they actually forbid it?

NAPOLEON HILL:

Unfortunately, for some people that is true, but the fact still remains that the big successes in life are based on the habit of Going the Extra Mile. If Henry Ford had not gone the extra mile, there would have been no Ford automobile and no Ford industrial empire, which gives employment directly and indirectly to many millions of people, some of whom now discourage the habit of Going the Extra Mile. If Thomas Edison had not gone the extra mile when he was working on the incandescent electric lamp, there would be no electrical equipment and no great electrical power and manufacturing companies, which now provide employment for millions of people. Think this over, and you will catch a glimpse of the importance of the habit of Going the Extra Mile.

ALDERFER:

This brings us to number four of the more important success principles, and I believe it is very closely tied in with the other three you have just discussed.

NAPOLEON HILL:

You have reference to the Master Mind Principle, through the application of which we can make use of the education, the experience, and the services of other people in carrying out our objectives in life. No great success is possible except by the combined efforts of many people, and this combination, this bringing together of many minds in a spirit of friendly coordination, is known as the Master Mind Principle.

ALDERFER:

For example, Thomas Edison could never have become the greatest inventor of all time if he had not used the education and experience of other people.

NAPOLEON HILL:

That is correct. Mr. Edison chose a calling that made it necessary for him to use most all of the sciences, yet he himself understood none of them. He bridged this deficiency by associating with men who did understand the sciences. And we witnessed this miracle from a man who had only three months of formal schooling, but who mastered this handicap and became the world's greatest inventor. Henry Ford, too, had only a limited common school education. He bridged his deficiency by surrounding himself with men who could do all the things he wanted done but that he couldn't do alone. Mr. Ford's greatest asset was his great capacity to know what he wanted and his persistence in sticking to his purpose through failure until he found success.

ALDERFER:

Wasn't it Henry Ford who said, "Taking the path of least resistance is what makes all rivers and some men crooked"?

NAPOLEON HILL:

Yes, I have heard him say that. And he made another statement that all of us would do well to remember. Many years ago he was on the witness stand as a witness in a libel suit he brought against a newspaper that called him an ignoramus. The lawyers for the newspaper were giving him a pretty hard time by asking him academic questions he could not answer, in order that they might prove he was ignorant. Finally, Mr. Ford got tired of this embarrassment. In reply to a particularly obnoxious question he leaned over, pointed his finger at the lawyer, and said, "If I should wish to answer the foolish question you have just asked, or any question I might need to have answered in the conduct of my business, all I have to do is put my finger on a push button, and in will come men who can give me the answer immediately. Now, will you tell me why I should clutter up my mind trying to remember how to answer questions when I have men all around me, some of them college-trained, who can do my answering for me?"

ALDERFER:

I suppose that put the lawyer in his place, didn't it?

NAPOLEON HILL:

Yes, and it did more than that. It gave me an idea that I wrote into some of my success books that now inspire people throughout the world to make use of the Master Mind Principle to which Mr. Ford referred. I studied Henry Ford very carefully for more than twenty years, and my observation of him disclosed that his huge success was due in the main to his application of two of the success principles we have presented on this program—Definiteness of Purpose and the Master Mind.

ALDERFER:

Now that we are approaching another anniversary of our Independence Day here in the United States, may it not be well if we all remember that it was the application of the Master Mind Principle that gave us our Declaration of Independence, with its far-flung influence on civilization throughout the world?

NAPOLEON HILL:

Yes, the fifty-six brave men who signed the Declaration of Independence definitely made use of the Master Mind Principle. Moreover, every man who signed this historic document well knew that he risked both his fortune and his life in doing so, because, if the American Revolution had failed, every signer of the Declaration would likely have been hanged as a traitor.

ALDERFER:

In the light of what has happened during the past few years, with men like Alger Hiss holding high places in our government and giving away our secrets to foreign enemies, one can't help wondering if we still have patriotic citizens who would risk their lives for the security of their country, as did the signers of the Declaration of Independence.

NAPOLEON HILL:

Yes, I believe we do have citizens as brave and as honest as those who signed the Declaration of Independence, and they will stand up to be counted if and when we are again overtaken by a national emergency such as that which existed in 1776. We always hear of the few who are dishonest because their reprehensible deeds make exciting front-page news, whereas those who are honest are taken for granted. We don't hear much about them, except in the obituary columns, after they pass on.

ALDERFER:

That is one very sound reason why this program features those who are helping to make this a better world by rendering useful service.

Which brings us to another success principle, that of Creative Vision, or Imagination.

NAPOLEON HILL:

Men and women with creative vision have always been the forerunners of human progress in every field of endeavor. Right now we need people with creative vision to give us a great many things that will make this a better world in which to live. For example, we need newspaper features that will turn the imagination of children to decency in conduct instead of crime. We need schoolteachers who will use imagination in teaching students how to read and, above all, how to think. We need someone with a keen imagination to give us a new code of conduct for automobile drivers so they will be as courteous to one another on the highways as they are in their homes.

ALDERFER:

Yes, I see what you mean. More importantly, we need protection from machine guns, jet-propelled airplanes laden with atomic bombs, and mad men who seem bent on destroying us all at one fell swoop. Here, then, is the need for creative vision that challenges the wisest brains that civilization has to offer.

NAPOLEON HILL:

Yes, civilization now faces its greatest challenge since the days of the caveman, with his sharpened stone weapons and his vicious will to kill without cause or reason.

ALDERFER:

Can you, with your keen imagination, envision a practical means by which man may once more regain his high place in civilization for which the Creator designed him? Can you foresee a practical means of meeting the challenge of the A-bomb and the H-bomb in the hands of men who seem determined to loose these destructive devices on the world?

NAPOLEON HILL:

Henry, it doesn't require a very keen imagination for one to recognize that there is but one means of meeting this newly developed challenge. The answer is not to be found by meeting armed force with armed force. It is not to be found by an arms race designed to give one nation superiority over another. It is not to be found in the air above us, nor in the sea beneath us. It is not to be found on the battlefield, for it has been proved over and over again that this method of settling differences among men only results in the conquered of today becoming the victors of tomorrow.

ALDERFER:

Evidently, from what you have just said, your imagination leads you to the conclusion that the solution to differences of beliefs and motives among men cannot be reached permanently by warfare. What, then, is the solution as you see it?

NAPOLEON HILL:

Listen, and I will tell you. Listen carefully please, all of you, for you have a responsibility that all of us must share, no matter who you are or what may be your beliefs. The safety of mankind, the survival of the gains of civilization we have made, depends upon the application of the Master Mind Principle in which we will start thinking, speaking, and living in terms of the Sermon on the Mount. Each of us can start right where he stands by relating himself to all those nearest him, on the basis of the Golden Rule. And this means tolerance of the views of others, in most cases, not coercion intended to change those views.

ALDERFER:

Do you sincerely believe that the salvation of civilization is as simple as that? Do you believe that all individuals will ever have a motive sufficiently strong to induce them to live by the Golden Rule other than when it seems expedient for their own purposes to do so, just as most people are doing and always have done?

NAPOLEON HILL:

Let me answer you this way: Everywhere throughout this nation people are being coached and trained in the art of defense for when the bombs begin to fall on this nation. And there is perhaps not an intelligent person who does not believe that he will live to see the day when whole cities will be wiped out in a matter of seconds, with thousands of people dying as the result of but a single bomb. Now tell me, don't you think that this is motive enough to cause people to begin looking beyond the powers of man for salvation against this mass form of murder?

ALDERFER:

Perhaps I am too much of a realist, and you are too much of an idealist for us to agree on such an important matter, but let me put it this way: Don't you believe that most people will begin turning to a power above man only after the bombs begin to fall? You know of course that Japan was warned that her cities would be wiped out unless she surrendered immediately, but not until two of her cities felt the blast of the atom bomb did she heed the warning.

NAPOLEON HILL:

I see your implication, and in most instances I would accept it, but in this case I do not agree with you. For it is true that God moves in a mysterious way with the power that created man and placed him on this little earth for a purpose that will not permit him to commit suicide because of his lack of wisdom as to the proper use of the newly discovered devices of destruction.

ALDERFER:

In other words, your imagination tells you that the A-bomb and the H-bomb may turn out to be blessings instead of curses? Is this your reasoning?

NAPOLEON HILL:

Not only my reasoning, but my Applied Faith. You see, I have graduated after having gone through more than forty years of testing of my personal faith, and I am now in a position to say that information I received from within, through my capacity for faith, is more reliable than that which I get through my reasoning powers. And may I say that I not only believe, but I know, that the world we live in today will find a way to survive the destructive devices man has conceived.

ALDERFER:

I concede that if everyone had the same capacity for faith that you express, we would have no A-bomb problems. In fact, we would have no problems of any sort that we could not solve through cooperation. But I am looking at the world, and at mankind from where we stand today—this very moment—and the picture is not as reassuring to me as it is to you.

NAPOLEON HILL:

Perhaps if you had been blessed with my background and my myriad testings of my faith, you would see the world as I see it. Of course, you know the philosopher foresees what lies in the future by examining what has happened in the past. In looking backward at the evolution of man, we can see that the all-wise Creator has provided a system that gives mankind a great leader when civilization is threatened by unusual emergencies. Often this leader emerges as an unknown, like the immortal Lincoln or George Washington. And I have faith that the answer to our present emergency will come forth when we are ready for it, just as have always been the experiences of the past.

ALDERFER:

Apparently you believe that the person or persons who will give us a remedy for the prevailing fears of total destruction through the A-bomb now lives and is in training for the job.

NAPOLEON HILL:

Yes, I do believe this, and I wouldn't have to tax my imagination too severely if I said I know that the plan and the person who will inspire the world to embrace and use it now exist.

ALDERFER:

Do you believe that the person who is destined to give us a remedy for the A-bomb now recognizes his mission?

NAPOLEON HILL:

Perhaps he doesn't. But that is unimportant, because he will know it when the people are ready. I doubt that Abraham Lincoln recognized the great responsibility ahead of him when he was being tested by one failure after another before he became president. And I can speak with authority when I tell you that I did not recognize the part I was destined to play in helping men and women to find themselves through personal success when I, myself, was meeting with failure after failure. It has been my observation that the Creator has not planned for individuals to be notified in advance when they have been chosen to render a great service in times of great emergencies.

ALDERFER:

I think we can sum up what you have been saying by stating that you are strongly advocating that men and women get back to living by their religion instead of merely belonging to a church and professing to believe in the Creator.

NAPOLEON HILL:

I couldn't have stated my belief in fewer or more expressive words, Henry. I sincerely believe that the world is about to undergo a great dramatic spiritual change in which each of us will feel it a great blessing, not merely a duty, to become his brother's keeper. Now, as always, before this change is final many people may be forced to shed tears of blood, but their struggles will give them the strength and the wisdom to recognize the difference between truth and falsehood. For more than thirty years, ever since my publication of the *Golden Rule Magazine*, right after World War I, I have been advocating the Golden Rule as the only sound foundation on which to succeed in business and professional relations. And I have observed that wherever this rule was adopted, the individuals who did so enjoyed outstanding success.

ALDERFER:

One thing we can all agree on is that we are living in a very sick world that is badly in need of a doctor, and if we are not sure that the answer to our problem lies in the adoption and use of the Golden Rule, we nevertheless know that the answer does not consist in mass murder through warfare, because we have seen this remedy fail every time it has been used.

NAPOLEON HILL:

A few years ago I saw an experiment tried out in Paris, Missouri, that convinced me that the Sermon on the Mount was the answer to all of our problems. I saw a group of men and women get together and form an organization that operated on the basis of mutual inspiration and cooperation. Within a year their influence had extended to at least a dozen surrounding towns and villages, where people began to experience prosperity such as they had never known before. The basis of the group's activities were the success principles we have been presenting on these programs.

ALDERFER:

I might add that these people in Paris, Missouri, are still using these success principles so effectively that many of them are experiencing success such as they never dreamed possible. I have met some of these people personally, and I have heard their stories from their own lips, and they have rededicated themselves to the application of the principles laid down by the Nazarene in the Sermon on the Mount. Do unto others as if you were the others. And not, do to others and do to them plenty, before they do you, as some people seem to believe the Golden Rule should be applied.

Thank you, Napoleon Hill, for your very interesting and inspiring discussions on the principles of success, here in Chicago. Sadly, our radio series must come to an end with today's program. Thank you also to our large and devoted audience of radio listeners.

NAPOLEON HILL:

Thank you, Henry, and thank you to our radio audience. I hope and trust that you will apply the success principles we have presented during these thirteen weeks, so that you may become truly successful and happy and enjoy peace of mind.

△

WISDOM TO LIVE BY

1. The Golden Rule means, substantially, to do unto others as you would wish them to do unto you if your positions were reversed.

2. Understand this rule and you will find it impossible to injure another person by thought or deed without injuring yourself.

3. The Golden Rule philosophy, when rightly understood and applied, not only makes dishonesty impossible, but it also makes impossible all other destructive qualities such as selfishness, greed, envy, bigotry, hatred, and malice. One is honest not out of the desire to be just with others, but because of the desire to be just with oneself.

ADVERSITY AND ADVANTAGE

1. It is a fact that each individual is the maker of their own destiny; and that one's thoughts and acts are the tools with which one does the making. Every act and every thought you release modifies your own character in exact conformity with the nature of the act or thought. Code of conduct is the sum total of one's thoughts and actions one lives by.

2. Napoleon Hill talks about his code of conduct in the Law of Success with which he lived himself. By applying this code to your own life every day, you will be on the sure path toward peace of mind, abundance, and success in your personal and professional life.

NAPOLEON HILL'S
CODE OF ETHICS

1. I believe in the Golden Rule as the basis of all human conduct; therefore, I will never do to another person that which I would not want done to me if our positions were reversed.

2. I will be honest, even to the slightest details, in all my transactions with others, not alone because of my desire to be fair with them, but because of my desire to impress the idea of honesty on my own subconscious mind, thereby weaving this essential quality into my own character.

3. I will forgive those who are unjust toward me, with no thought as to whether they deserve it or not, because I understand the law through which forgiveness of others strengthens my own character and wipes out the effects of my own transgressions, in my own subconscious mind.

4. I will be just, generous, and fair with others always, even though I know that these acts will go unnoticed and unrewarded in the ordinary terms of reward, because I understand that one's own character is but the sum total of one's own acts and deeds.

5. Whatever time I may have to devote to the discovery and exposure of the weaknesses and faults of others, I will devote more profitably to the discovery and correction of my own.

6. I will slander no person, no matter how much I may believe another person may deserve it, because I wish to plant no destructive suggestion in my own subconscious mind.

7. I recognize the power of thought as being an inlet leading into my brain from the universal ocean of life; therefore, I will set no destructive thoughts afloat upon that ocean, lest they pollute the minds of others.

8. I will conquer the common human tendency toward hatred, and envy, and selfishness, and jealousy, and malice, and pessimism, and doubt, and fear; for I believe these to be the seeds from which the world harvests most of its troubles.

9. When my mind is not occupied with thoughts that tend toward the attainment of my definite chief aim in life, I will voluntarily keep it filled with thoughts of courage, and self-confidence, and goodwill toward others, and faith, and kindness, and loyalty, and the love for the truth, and justice, for I believe these to be the seeds from which the real world reaps its harvest of progressive growth.

10. I understand that a mere passive belief in the soundness of Golden Rule philosophy is of no value whatsoever, either to myself or to others; therefore, I will actively put into operation this universal rule for good in all my transactions with others.

11. I understand that my character is developed from my own acts and thoughts; therefore, I will guard with care all that goes into its development.

12. Realizing that enduring happiness comes only through helping others find it, that no act of kindness is without its reward even though it may never be directly repaid, I will do my best to assist others when and where the opportunity appears.

The time for practicing the Golden Rule philosophy is upon us. In business as well as in social relationships, he who neglects or refuses to use the Golden Rule as the basis of his dealings will certainly meet failure.

APPENDIX

UNIDENTIFIED SPEAKER:

This is the first fall meeting of the Chicago Dental Research Club at the Germania Club. The date is Wednesday, September 24, 1952. The speaker today is Napoleon Hill, and the subject is Better Living.

We have with us today a member of our own profession who has had much in common with our speaker of the day. His background in knowing the speaker so well gives me the feeling that I would like at this time to introduce to you Dr. Straub, who will introduce our speaker.

DR. STRAUB:

Thank you. It has been my privilege and extreme pleasure during the last year, year and a half now, to know our speaker real well. I never would have thought several years ago when I first took a college course and read on the first page of the practice manual references to Napoleon Hill's *Think and Grow Rich*, that I'd ever meet the man, let alone eat with him, have him in my office, and last night have him in my home. But I wondered when I first read *Think and Grow Rich*, as everybody else does, what kind of a man writes this thing? Some of it is so fabulous that it's hard to believe, and immediately you begin to get the feeling that I'd like to meet this man and know how he thinks, how he gets these ideas to put into a book like *Think and Grow Rich*.

Last November Dr. Hancock called me about four o'clock in the afternoon, and he said, "Napoleon Hill's at St. Louis tonight." And that's all he said. St. Louis is 150 miles from me. I said, "Everett, are you going over?" He said, "Yeah." I said, "I'll be there. When are you leaving?" So he gave me about fifty minutes to get seventy-five miles to his office in Salem, and we heard Napoleon Hill in St. Louis that night. We took his course that he gave in St. Louis. Everett recorded it, all of it. We've played the recording I suppose a dozen times. Through the efforts of Dr. Hancock, Dr. Hill was persuaded to come to Salem and give a course. So I drove to Salem once a week for about three months or so and went through the course twice. By accident or by design, I don't know which yet exactly, we have a little manufacturing plant in Fairfield that was having a lot of labor difficulties. I asked Dr. Hill about it and introduced some of the men from this plant to him. This month, Dr. Hill is in Fairfield trying to straighten out some of these labor difficulties in this plant, and I think before it's through you will hear a lot about the Sheppard Manufacturing Company in Fairfield, because I think they're going to have a fine personnel relationship before they're through.

As far as Dr. Hill's work with dentistry, his father was a dentist, and he's very familiar with a lot of the dental problems of dentists and dental patients. He sat in my office. I tell him a lot of my problems, and we discuss them. I know he has a lot to give you, but Dr. Hill digs right into the meat of everything when he starts. So I want everybody, if you will, do me the honor and the privilege just to hang on for the first thirty minutes, because I can promise you an exciting talk. We flew in last night, but I'm going to go a lot higher today with Dr. Hill than I went last night.

Without any further introduction, I'd like at this time to present Napoleon Hill, author of *Think and Grow Rich, Mental Dynamite, The Law of Success,* and several other volumes I'll not go into, and this morning he showed us a manuscript for a new book, *How to Condition a Dental Patient's Mind for Dentistry.* Dr. Hill.

NAPOLEON HILL:

Mr. President, gentlemen. You know this group of men sitting around this table with this opportunity that I have to speak to them on such an intimate basis reminds me of the story that I heard once about the distinguished evangelist Sam Jones. A parishioner came in one day and he said, "Father, I hear you talking a lot about God. Do you mind if I ask you some questions about God?" Sam said, "Why no, son. Go right ahead. Ask me any question you choose. I think I do know a lot about God." He said, "Well, Father, who made God?" Sam said, "Now look here, my son. I have the answer to that all right, but the trouble with you is that you don't have anything to put it in."

The reason I looked forward to this talk with a great deal of anticipation is that if I wouldn't find a group of men here who have something to put it in, I frankly wouldn't know where to go to look for them. I don't much care for mixed audiences made up of housewives, women and men, and businessmen, professional men, and all that sort of thing because you have to generalize your talk so much that you don't hardly get anything across. It's like a modern kimono. It spreads all over you and doesn't reveal anything.

I'm going to talk mostly on the subject of mental attitude because I consider this to be the most important thing in the world. To begin with, there is only one thing that any person has complete control over, complete unchallenged and unchallengeable control. That's not your wife, nor your bank account, nor your profession, and certainly not your patients. But there is one thing that you control 100 percent, and that's the privilege of controlling your mental attitude and making it whatever you choose to have it be. You can make it positive or you can make it negative. And I take it for granted that the Creator or whoever it was that made man, in giving him control over but one thing, intended that that should be the most important thing in the world, and I contend that it is the most important thing because I have observed that those who exercise that great privilege and project their minds to definite objectives are the men who succeed, and the people who do not exercise that are the men who go down in defeat.

I have never yet known any person who exercised the full privilege of using his own mind and making his mental attitude positive that didn't succeed in whatever he started out to do, and I'm going to give you illustration after illustration today, many of them with which you are familiar, that will indicate that the outstanding men, the thing that makes men outstanding, is that they are capable of taking charge of their own mind and making that mind positive instead of negative.

I want to give you an illustration that I think will enrich you of a positive mental attitude on the part of the greatest woman I have ever met.

There have been many women in my life, I can assure you, many of them. I married four of them. Now don't misunderstand me. Most of these women I know have been students of mine. I know a great deal about women, I think. Of course, all men think that. But there was one woman in my life who stood out like a sore thumb. She was the first one who came into my life at the rich old age, at the ripe old age of nine years. She was my stepmother. And when my father introduced her to me, she made a speech that has reverberated around this world that has already influenced over sixty-five million of people for the better, I hope, and is destined to benefit millions yet unborn. One short speech.

My father introduced her all around the room to the relatives who had gathered the night that he brought her home and finally came to me. I was standing over in the corner with my chin down on my chest looking tough and trying to hate this terrible woman that my aunts had told me was coming to take my mother's place. Made up my mind I was not going to like her at all. My father finally got around to me, and he said, "And, Martha, over here in the corner is your son, Napoleon, the meanest boy in Wise County." And I straightened up and tried to look and feel the part of a mean boy. She marched over and put her hand under my chin and lifted my head up and looked right squarely into my eyes, and she turned on my father and made this famous speech. She said, "You're wrong about this boy. You're just as wrong as you can be. He's not the meanest boy in Wise County. He's just the smartest boy in Wise County who hasn't yet found out what to do with his smartness." And that moment, gentlemen, I knew that my stepmother and I were going to get along all right. I had intended to become a second Jesse James, only I intended to shoot straighter and more often than he did until I met my stepmother, and her positive mental attitude got into my blood.

The next thing that happened, about two weeks after she and father were married, she was getting breakfast one morning and she dropped her denture and broke it; an upper plate. I had never seen a denture up to that time. I didn't know there was such a thing. Of course, I found out a lot about it since. My father went over and picked up those pieces and reassembled them in his hand and looked at them for a moment. He said, "Martha, you know, I believe I can make a set of teeth." She dropped those pots and pans right over there and grabbed him around the neck and kissed him and said, "Well I know you can make a set of teeth." And I thought, *What a woman; my old man make a set of teeth! Why, he can shoe a horse,* I'd seen him do that, but I knew he would never be able to make a set of teeth.

About a month later I came home from school, and when I got in the yard, I smelled an odor that I couldn't isolate. I never had smelled anything like this; smelled even worse than a skunk, and when I got in the house, I saw a queer little kettle sitting over the fire cooking. I said to my stepmother, "What is that?" She said, "Well that's a set of teeth. We sent away and got a vulcanizer. We got some plaster of Paris. We got some teeth and your father made an impression of my mouth, and he's got the teeth in there cooking now." I thought, *What a woman! What a woman!*

Well in a little while they took the kettle off and we went down to the river to cool it down so we could open it up, and when this hunk of plaster of Paris and rubber came out it was about so big, and I thought, *My God, they'll never get that in my stepmother's mouth.* They shaved away that plaster, and that excess rubber was cut away with the fine end of a horse rasp. I don't know whether you know what a horse rasp is. A horse rasp is a file that you cut away the excess part of the hoof with after you put the shoe on. He took that fine edge of that and smoothed this plate down. Then he took a piece of sandpaper and sanded the plate down, and then came the big moment. He put the thing in my stepmother's mouth, and believe you-me, it fitted almost perfectly, and she wore it for three years, and presto, the next time I came back from school I saw a great big sign hanging across the front of our house, Dr. J. M. Hill, Dentist. She had made a dentist out of him overnight, and he started practicing, and everything that he used in the way of tools and equipment he made. He made a pair of forceps that would—I'll tell you they were honeys for pulling teeth. They had no anesthetics or anything of that sort. To pull teeth you put a man down in the chair and put two strong men, one on each shoulder and one to hold his feet, and you simply got the teeth out.

He went to practicing down through the mountains of Virginia and Kentucky, traveling on horseback and was really doing fine when one day the local justice of the peace came down with a great big law book under his arm. "Now lookee here, Dr. Hill, look here what it says under Section 560 Code of Virginia. It says you've got to have a license to practice dentistry, and if you don't have, you're liable to go to jail and pay a fine." Well, they went into a huddle, and my father finally decided to go out to the county courthouse to see a lawyer, see what could be done about it, and on his way back, I could tell by the way he was riding on the horse that he'd been licked; and as he got off his horse, my stepmother made another famous speech that I'll never forget, gentlemen, as long as I live. He said, "Martha, it's all off. The lawyer tells me that I can't get a license without I take an examination. Of course, you know I can't do that. I don't have enough education." She said, "Now, lookee here, Dr. Hill, I didn't make a dentist out of you to have you let me down. If you have to take an examination, then you go to college and take it just like everybody else does." And I thought, *my oh my, the way the college was, they wouldn't let him on the campus ground, let alone in college.* But he did go to college. He settled down at Louisville Dental College for four years and paid his tuition and expenses with the life insurance money of her former husband. I'd say today that was very good economics.

Gentlemen, he won every medal until the last year; they wouldn't let him try for the highest medal because they knew he would win it. You see, he knew more about dentistry when he went in there than most of them do when they came out because he'd been out in the field practicing. I don't know whether this story that I'm telling you is any compliment to your profession or not, but I'm just telling what one man did with it. But it wasn't the man that did it; it was the mental attitude of that woman that could lay it out for him. When the woman of your choice gets back of you and becomes determined to put you across; you'd better get across. It's the simplest thing to do. I know because I have one of that kind now. I had three others that didn't do anything to put me across, and as a result, well, I don't have them anymore.

Now I ought to give you an illustration of mental attitude that is right up your alley. Came a time when I had to have my teeth taken out. I didn't particularly dread that time because I had been around dentists. My father was a dentist and one of my uncles was a dentist. I had become pretty conscious to it early in life. But I did know that taking out all of your teeth by surgery was a major operation. And before I started to have my dental work done, I spent three days conditioning my mind so that I would not only go through that without any unpleasantness, but I would make it a marvelous interlude, an interlude in which I would prove to myself that I could sit down and have my teeth taken out without not only having any unpleasantness but enjoying it.

I went down to the dentist that I thought would do the job properly and became acquainted with him and cultivated him for about a week and got him properly conditioned before he started in on the work. Then he turned me over to a man who did nothing but extraction work. He took out all of my teeth at one sitting except nine. He left nine of them. There's five above and four below. It wasn't unpleasant because I had conditioned my mind not to let it be unpleasant, and when I went back to have these nine teeth taken out, he gave me the anesthetic in the upper and lower jaw of course, and my jaw and my whole face was numb, and he was fumbling around in my mouth examining. Every minute or two he'd look in there. I thought he was waiting for the anesthetic to take effect. Finally, in a little while I said, "Well doctor, aren't you about ready to start taking those teeth out?" He said, "What do you mean am I not ready? I've already taken them all out but three, and there they are on the table." And sure enough, there they were. I had so thoroughly disassociated myself from what I was actually doing. In my mind, I was at the radio station rehearsing my following Sunday's program entirely separated from that operation. Now that's what you can do with your mental attitude if you make up your mind and do it. You can put your mind where you want it to be and not let anything interfere with that operation.

Some of you have read *Think and Grow Rich*. It undoubtedly leads all books of its kind for popularity, and now in its fifteenth year, it has sold in foreign countries alone over ten million copies and it is selling all over the world better than it did when it came out or ever has since. I want to give you the story of that book briefly because it has a direct bearing on the subject of mental attitude. I wrote that book and six other books while I was working for Franklin D. Roosevelt during his first term. It was my job to sell that ill-fated NRA. May God forgive me. And in between times when I wasn't out in the country speaking on that subject, I was writing books to keep from going crazy, like so many other people I saw around me. We were all in a stampede of fear, you know, and I wanted to keep out of that, and in order to do it, to keep my mind positive I started writing books. I didn't intend to publish the books. I was just writing to keep myself out of mischief. In 1936 I got all seven of these books done. I soon discovered there was something radically wrong with *Think and Grow Rich*, and you'll be surprised when I tell you what it was, because that something that was wrong with it that I discovered was the thing today that has made it a bestseller all over the world, has made it a book that has probably made more successful men than any book that was ever written, meaning by that, money success. When I read this manuscript, gentlemen, I found out that the tempo of it was too slow. It was written in a tempo of fear. I had caught the spirit of this tremendous fear that we were all in. We were millions of people who were releasing thoughts of fear, and I had tuned in and picked that up and had written my book in that tempo.

I sat down to my typewriter. I didn't change a word in it. I sat down to my typewriter and typed that book entirely in a new enthusiastic frame of mind, with a Positive Mental Attitude, and that's the thing that gave that book that magic touch. Now when you read the book it doesn't tell you anything new. There isn't a thing new in it, but what it does, it causes you to go back in your mind and take the things that you already use and start doing something about them, and that's what most of us need. We don't need more education or more knowledge or more facts or more opportunities. We need to make the best of the opportunities we already have. We're living in the greatest country that's ever been known to civilization. What we need is to embrace our birthing here and start making use of our abilities in a way that we're not doing now.

I have faced many circumstances in life where I had to keep my attitude positive or else. During my forty-odd years of experience in organizing the Science of Success, I have undergone at least twenty major defeats or failures, at least twenty of them. The only effect that any of them had on me was to cause me to come back fighting, with a determination that I would not accept from life anything I didn't want. That's quite a bold statement, and, parenthetically, before I proceed I want to tell you that you are now looking at a man who has everything in this world that he wants, as much of it as he needs, including peace of mind, and I have never accepted from life anything I didn't want.

I married three different women that didn't suit. I got rid of them. I traded them in on a better model until I finally found one that did suit—or maybe one or two of them traded me in. Now don't get any ideas from what I've said like trying to trade in your wives; you might make a mistake.

The extreme test of my entire life came when my second son was born. Doctors who brought him into the world met me out in the outer room of the hospital and said, "Well now, young fellow, we want to prepare you for a shock. Your son was born without any ears. He has no sign of ears, and of course, he will be deaf and dumb all his life. You may just as well know that now. There are children born that way, and not in the history of medicine have we ever known of one to learn to hear." I said, "Doctor, my son may have been born without ears, but I am telling you, sir, that he will not go through life a deaf and dumb mute." One of the doctors came over and took me by the shoulder and said, "Now brace up. Take it easy, fella. You have to learn that there are some things in this world that you have to accept, and this is one of them." I said, "I will never accept it."

I went to work on that child before I ever saw him. I worked on him sometimes as much as three hours during the night, giving him directives through his subconscious mind, with a strong mental attitude directed to his brain with determination that I was going to influence Nature to improvise for him a hearing system. And up to about the end of the third year, there were no signs that anything had happened, and then about that time we commenced to notice that I was getting through to him. I could wake him up without saying a word, without going into the room just by commanding him to wake up, and by the time he was nine years of age, he had gone through the grade schools, and by the time he was twenty years of age he had gone through college. We found that, at about the age of nine, he had been restored to 65 percent of his normal hearing.

Then I took him up to the company that manufactures the acoustic hearing aids and they built him a special hearing aid that gave him 100 percent of his hearing, and then they sent him all over the country speaking before medical groups and dental groups, and so forth. But before they would take a chance on doing that, they had some of the most outstanding experts on ears to take x-rays of him. They must've made 150, 200 x-rays. One of the doctors was the famous Dr. Irving Vorhees of New York City, and I asked him, I said, "Doctor, my son has 65 percent of his hearing, and you say that the test showed he can hear things that you and I can't hear. He hears sounds that you and I can't hear. What do you think is responsible? Why is he different from all other people who have been found in that condition?" He said, "Well undoubtedly the psychological directives that you gave him caused Nature to improvise some sort of a hearing system; probably a new set of nerves connected to some portion of the brain to the inner walls of his skull enabling him to hear, what we now call bone conduction."

My son went through college. He's gone through life up to the present time very well adjusted. I adjusted him in the very beginning to take this attitude toward his affliction that it was not something to be worried about. I said, "You'll get through life a lot easier than your brothers because people will see your condition, and they will be kind to you," and that's exactly what's happened. My greatest effort was not in conditioning his mind to take the positive side in reference to his affliction, it was to keep his mother and his aunt and his grandmother from sending him down to one of these places where you learn the sign language and where you learn lip-reading and all that sort of thing. I didn't want him to find out about such concessions. I wanted him to learn to trust upon that thing that comes from within, because I have found out that if you want to get a good grip on this God-given thing that you have, this only thing that you have control of, that you'll use it and rely upon it. It will come to your aid on every occasion and for every purpose.

I ought to know about that because if you could mention a circumstance of defeat that I haven't experienced or gone through, I'd like to know what it is, and I have never yet known this faith, this ability to rely upon your own mind power, to let you down.

In my work I have naturally come into contact with many famous outstanding men, but I don't believe in all my experience I have ever known one who was more interesting to me than the late Mahatma Gandhi of India. It was through Gandhi's influence that my book *Think and Grow Rich* was first introduced there, and later all of my books. Over three and a half million copies of *Think and Grow Rich* alone have been sold in India. Mahatma Gandhi was an outstanding figure, and he always intrigued me because of the marvelous things that he did with his mind. Now, he didn't have any soldiers. He didn't have any money. He didn't have a house to live in. He didn't even have a pair of britches. And yet he licked the great British Empire and freed the people of India through what he called passive resistance.

Passive resistance is nothing in the world but taking an attitude that you're not going to accept what you don't want, just as I did with reference to my son. I never did accept that affliction as being something that couldn't be remedied. Gandhi never did accept the control of the British government over his people as being something that couldn't be undone. He indoctrinated over 200 million of his fellow men with that passive resistance, that idea of holding a positive mental attitude toward the things they wanted in life until eventually the British government collapsed, and India had her freedom. All as the result of the mental attitude of one man, just one man.

One of the other outstanding men that I worked with and who collaborated with me and who was largely responsible in testing many of these principles before they ever got into any of my books was the late Thomas A. Edison. I think the thing about Mr. Edison that intrigued me more than anything else was his method and his system of positioning his mind to refuse to accept defeat when he was experimenting with his inventions. When he was working on the incandescent electric light, for instance, which was his first outstanding invention, he met with over ten thousand separate and distinct failures before he finally found the answer. Think of a man going through ten thousand failures and not quitting and deciding that he wanted to do something else.

Do you have any idea, gentlemen, how many times the average man has to be defeated about anything before he quits? Give a guess. How many times the average man has to be defeated before he quits, no matter what the importance of these objectives may be. Give a guess. No, it isn't even once because a lot of them quit before they start. I saw his log books in which these failures were recorded. On every page there was a separate description of a separate thing he tried that didn't work. There were two stacks of them that high. Each book had about 200 failures in it. Years of work, and when I was talking to Mr. Edison one day about it, I said, "Mr. Edison, what would you have done if after the ten-thousandth try you hadn't found the answer? What would you be doing now?" He said, "Well I'd be right in my laboratory working instead of out here fooling away my time talking to you." And that's just what he would've been doing.

I want to tell you, gentlemen, that the most astounding thing that I discovered in working with more than 500 of the most outstanding men of this nation who developed the business philosophies, including Mr. Edison and Mr. Ford, the thing that I discovered about them that was astounding was that they didn't have a blessed thing on the face of this earth in the way of ability that you and I don't have. They just made better use of what they have than you and I are making. That was the only difference. The thing that enabled Edison to wrestle from Nature the secrets that he did bring forth was his determination not to accept defeat, and I know that this is true. I have no orthodox religion. I'm not an orthodox religionist. I'm not an atheist either, but it seems to me that the Creator or Infinite Intelligence or some great force throws itself on the side of the man who knows precisely what he wants and is determined to take nothing less.

I think it would be no overstatement of the fact if I said definitely that there is an overall power of some sort that comes to the rescue of a man whose mental attitude is such that no matter how many times he's knocked down, no matter how many defeats he meets with, he still says, I know where I'm going; I'm bound and determined I'm going to get that. But if you can take that kind of an attitude toward any kind of a problem, you'll find that there is a solution. There's no such thing in this world as a problem without a solution. All problems have solutions, albeit the solution at times is not the solution that the individual would want.

And then there is another thing about this question of a positive mental attitude that you have to know about before you can develop that kind of a habit. You have to recognize that every adversity, every defeat, every step back, every failure, every punishment carries with it the seed of an equivalent benefit. No exception to that rule. There never has been and there never will be.

I was talking to my students down at the Sheppard Manufacturing Company yesterday about that, and one of them said, "What about Nixon? Don't you think he's in a mess now? What's the seed of an equivalent benefit there to the Republican Party?" I seized that. I was just waiting for somebody to ask me a question like that, and it was one of the most outstanding examples that I could possibly give. I want to tell you that nothing has happened during his campaign as beneficial to the Republican Party as what has happened to Nixon, provided he comes clean, because people know him all over this country who never would've known him at all, and when the thing is over if he's on top, it would be the greatest blessing that ever came to the Republican Party. I hope and pray that he'll come clean, but if he does not, I still say, that seed of equivalent benefit is in the incident because I can say we will not have elected the wrong man.

I now want to tell you about the most interesting character I have ever known. And I hope that you do not jump to any false conclusions about my story until I have finished, when I tell you who this man is.

A good many years ago a little Black Alabama cotton field worker, who stands about that high, was leaning on his pole and mopping his brow and pondering over the reason for this vast difference between men who were born with White skins and men who were born with Black skins. And while he was standing there pondering over this subject, an idea hit him. Nobody knows exactly where this idea came from, but an idea hit him, and in connection with it he started putting into operation the most outstanding parts of the seventeen principles of the Science of Success that I've devoted my life to organizing. The first principle would be Definiteness of Purpose, knowing where you are going and being determined to get there. He laid down that pole and went back to the house and announced that suddenly he had become God on earth, and he gave himself the pseudonym of Father Divine. He got two or three other men together, and they started up north to put this marvelous new job of his into a better setting than they had down south. Before they got up to New York the two men that went along with him and had started, they both quit and had to go back to work. He finally got up there, and some ten years later when I was sent up there by a ministerial association to expose this imposter, show him up for what he was, I became acquainted with him and learned about his technique and learned what had happened. I was talking to him one day, and I said, "Now, Father Divine, I want to ask you a very personal question about this business of calling yourself God. Is that just a—you know that's a fake, don't you, but you're just doing it for publicity, aren't you? Give me the lowdown on that now. You've been frank about other things." He said, "Now look here, Mr. Hill. I will only talk about things we're apt to agree on." And I thought, *oh-oh*, and I commenced to look at that man from a different angle from that minute on.

He claims to have thirty million followers. He's wealthier than Henry Ford. He's the wealthiest preacher that ever lived on the face of this earth. He's been smarter than anybody sitting in this room, and he's never had to pay Uncle Sam a single dime in income taxes, and his money comes in without solicitation from White men and Black men. I don't know whether he has thirty million followers or not, but I wouldn't be at all surprised if he doesn't have at least ten or twelve million, part of them Whites, and I thought, *well these people are just a bunch of disappointed, frustrated nuts*, and I began to interview some of them. I want to tell you I got the surprise of my life. They weren't frustrated nuts at all. Many of them were quite intelligent people who said they had just gotten tired of the old orthodox way of doing things and thought they'd give this upstart a good chance and went over, joining.

So I went back and reported to the ministerial association that sent me up there. I said, "Listen, if I'd have stood up there another thirty days I'd have joined him probably." The point that I want to make, gentlemen, is that because of the part of the country in which he was born and on account of his color, there were two strikes against him to start with, and you and I know that. There wasn't a chance on the face of this earth theoretically of him ever becoming financially independent. Not a chance. And yet he came up out of the South. He made himself immensely wealthy. He's immensely wealthy today and is still rolling on. What happened? Something happened that he took possession of his own mind, and I think that whoever it is that manages things out there in the cosmos doesn't care if the mind is under a colored skin or under a White skin. A mind is a mind, and when a man discovers that he has a mind, makes it positive, directs it to things that are beneficial, and becomes determined to get the thing he goes after, he can succeed.

I have based my Science of Success philosophy upon the observation of many thousands of people, people who were down and out, and I've seen them lifted up again and sent on their way to success. Right after the end of the World War I, a young soldier came into my office one day, and he said, "Mr. Hill I'm down and out. I need a place to sleep tonight, and I need something to eat. I'm hungry." Well I said, "Come in, soldier. Let's sit down. Are you willing to settle for a sandwich and a place to room?" He said, "That's all I need right now." I said, "Let's not settle so cheaply.

Come in. Let's see if you can't get something more than this out of life." I spent two hours with him, at the end of which I found the only two assets he had that were marketable. I found that before he went to the war he had been working for the Fuller Brush Company and selling Fuller brushes very successfully, but something happened in the war that took away his confidence, and he didn't even have enough confidence to go back to the Fuller Brush Company when he got out. I found that while he was in the service, he did a lot of KP service and he learned to cook. Now those are the only two things he had. He could cook and he could sell. I said, "Soldier, instead of settling for a sandwich and a room, how'd you like to settle for a million dollars?" He said, "Now, lookee here, fella, I didn't come in here to be insulted." He said, "I'm hungry. Don't you understand what hunger means? Have you ever been hungry?" I said, "I've been hungry. Hungry for many things, for knowledge, for opportunity, for food." I said, "You can sell. You can cook. Let's put those two things together. Let's mastermind a little bit on this and see what we can work out of it."

I won't go into all of the details, but inside of a week I had set him up selling aluminum cookware. He'd go out into a neighborhood, get ahold of that housewife, and have her invite all of her neighbors in, and he'd cook the dinner on this aluminum cookware, and after dinner he'd take orders for the aluminum cookware. That was the sum and the substance of it. I took him out to my house and gave him a room. I sent him over to Marshall Fields, where I have a charge account, and got him some good clothing, and I gave him a couple hundred dollars advance in pocket money while he's getting started. First thing I knew, he had a dozen other people out working for him doing the same thing, and he's getting a commission on it. Next thing I knew he had forty or fifty salesmen and, all of a sudden, he dropped out of sight, and I didn't hear from him at all for almost four years, and he came in one day, walked up to me, and said, "Well Mr. Hill, I came back to pay off." I said, "What do you mean, come back to pay off?" He said, "You ought to know." Well, I said, "I don't know. I never saw you before in my life." Well, he said, "You saw me all right." He was all dressed up, and that awful dead look he had in his eye when I first met him was gone. He was a different man. He'd been reborn again. He said, "I'm that man that you set up in the cookware." "Oh," I said. "Don't tell me you are that man?" He said, "Yes, I'm the same man. I came back to pay off." And he reached down in his overcoat pocket to commence laying out bankbooks. I never saw so many bankbooks in all my life. The first one I picked up had a credit of $560,000 in it. Next one $300,000, and they ran like that, and finally I said, "Well, what are you showing me all this for?" He said, "I told you I'd come back to pay off." He had accounts in practically every city in the United States and he had a check in his pocket. He said, "I brought your check. I made the check out to you. I've signed it, and these books here say it's good up to $4 million, and all that money is mine. I want you to fill in the amount that you think that I owe you." I said, "Listen, I didn't do what I did for you for pay. I did it just to demonstrate that I had a philosophy that could take a man who was down and out and bring him up and put him on his feet again. I have already been paid for the opportunity that you gave me to show you how to get back on your own." I could see by the look of disappointment in his eyes that he's going to take an awful disappointment if I didn't take some money. So I took out my fountain pen. I said, "All right. I filled in $10,000 and handed it back and said, "How's that?" Well, he said, "All I can figure, if I were sitting over there where you are with all these books here in front of me, and I had a chance to fill in that check, brother, I wouldn't be as modest as you are. I'd make it for more."

That is the gentleman who started what now is a major industry, and there are at least half a dozen concerns throughout the United States like that, started by my students; among them the Century Metal Corporation, and one of the most outstanding of my students is the general manager of that concern, and he has over 250 salesmen working for him, and he takes a farm boy, almost any kind of boy and in a little while he had enough there making twenty, twenty-five thousand dollars a year. Every man who goes out has to take this philosophy. In other words, that's a must. He doesn't allow anyone to go into the field until he has been trained in this philosophy, with which the man's mind is conditioned to go out there and do the things he was sent out to do without taking no for an answer.

In 1908 my brother and I had matriculated in Georgetown University Law School in Washington, intending to go through school and become lawyers. We didn't have any money, but I did have the ability to write. My stepmother had trained me to become a correspondent for country newspapers. I agreed that I would earn the money by writing stories about successful men, selling them to magazines, and fortunately my first assignment was to interview Andrew Carnegie. He set aside three hours of his time for me. At the end of those three hours he said, "Well, young man, this interview is just starting. We are not done. You come on out to the house, and we'll take it up again at dinner." Well, I felt like a million dollars. Mr. Carnegie, the richest man in the world, and a youngster like me, and inviting me out to the house. I felt greatly honored. I couldn't understand it.

Well, after dinner he started in to tell me, he said, "Now it's a very commendable thing for you to go out writing stories about men like myself whom you call successful because they've accumulated a few million dollars." But he said, "What this country and what the world needs is a philosophy that will take the know-how gained by such men as myself from a lifetime of experience by the trial-and-error method, take that know-how and put it into a philosophy, a simple philosophy that the man on the street can understand, whereby he can succeed without making all of the mistakes in the book, such as we who have learned by the trials and errors like I have done." And then he went on to say that, "From the days of Plato and Socrates on down to the days of Emerson and William James we have had many philosophies, but they had all been abstract philosophies and dealing with the moral laws of life and not the economic laws of life." And he said, "What we need is a good, sound philosophy of individual achievement that will give a man all the know-how that there is available that other men have learned by a lifetime of experience."

Well, he drilled that into my mind, and he kept talking about it for three days and nights, and finally at the end of the time he said, "Now I've been talking to you for approximately three days about this new philosophy, and I'm going to ask you a question about it, and I want you to answer it with a yes or a no. I don't want you to answer until you make up your mind definitely whether it is a yes or a no. If I commission you to become the author of the world's first philosophy of success, introduce you to men of outstanding achievement, open doors to you all over this country so that you can get their story and get their collaboration, are you willing to devote twenty years of research to doing the job, for that's the time it will take, and earn your own way as you go along without any subsidy from me, yes or no?" Gentlemen, at that time there was only one other time in my life when I was so stunned and shocked and so near the collapsing point of saying that I couldn't do it. And that was when my son was born, and the news was spoken to me that he was without ears. I tried every way in the world to tell Mr. Carnegie why I couldn't accept it. In other words, I could think of a dozen things immediately, that "no can do" part of it immediately popped up, and I commenced thinking about it. I don't have the money. I don't have the education. I don't even know what the word *philosophy* means. All of the no-can-do part of the circumstance crept into my mind, and I was trying desperately hard to tell him that I couldn't do it, when inside of me something said, *well, if Mr. Carnegie, the most outstanding man in America, the best judge of men industry has ever known, has found in you something that justifies in him in giving you such a commission, you tell him you can do it.* Finally, I said, "Well, yes, Mr. Carnegie. I not only will accept the commission, sir, but you can depend upon me. I will complete it." He said, "The last part of your statement was what I wanted to hear. I also wanted to see the look in your eyes and hear the tone of your voice when you said that. You've got it." I learned later on, gentlemen, that he was sitting there with a stopwatch under his desk timing me. He had given me exactly sixty seconds in which to make up my mind after all the facts had been put before me, and he told me that I had consumed exactly twenty-nine seconds in telling him yes, and if I'd have gone the sixty seconds, I would have lost the opportunity of a lifetime.

I don't believe that any author in the history of the world at any time in my field and perhaps in any other field, I don't think any single author has had as much help and as much collaboration from so many outstanding men over so long a period of years as I have had, and when I went back to

Washington and told my brother what had happened, he got up and walked over and put his hand on my shoulder and came up real close and said, "You know, Napoleon, all of my life I hate to tell you this, but all of my life I thought you were weird, but from here on out, sir, I'll tell you that there are no doubts in my mind. I know that you are more than weird, and what you really ought to do is to go down to the psychopathic ward and have your damn head examined, because you're as crazy as hell. Going to work for the richest man in the world for twenty years without pay. What are you going to use for money?" Well, I swallowed. My mouth got dry, and it did look kind of silly because of the way he put it. It looked foolish. It did. And I thought, *maybe there is something wrong with me. Guess there is, but the deed's been done, and I'm going to stick by it.*

Two years ago in the very same room where my brother made that speech, he went on through Georgetown University Law School and became a rather successful lawyer. Two years ago in that very same room in the Willard Hotel he made another speech. He said, "A long time ago, my present wife and I were there together, a long time ago I made a speech to you in this room here, and it was a rather caustic speech. I now know I was wrong. Your books have made millions of dollars, and probably will gross fifty or sixty million dollars before it's through. *Think and Grow Rich* is selling better today than it did when it first came out and selling all over the world practically, and that one book alone has earned more money already than four generations of people on both sides of the family have earned." My brother said, "I certainly owe you an apology for the statements I made because you did stick by your guns through thick and thin."

I won't tell you what it took me to do that, gentlemen. There were times when I first started out when my closest relatives made fun of me and said, "Well, Napoleon Hill, teaching people how to succeed. He doesn't have two nickels to rub together of his own." And the worst part of it was they were telling the truth. Well, came the time when I got a couple of nickels and the privilege, probably, the privilege of rendering more practical, useful service to mankind than anybody who has ever written books in my field. And the thing that carried me through those twenty years, gentlemen, when I had to get my living in other ways, the thing that carried me through was the mental attitude that I said I had promised Mr. Carnegie—I will do this thing, and I don't care how long it takes. I don't care what the price is. I don't care how many obstacles I meet with. I don't care how many people criticize me. I will do it in spite of hell and high water, and speaking of hell and high water, there was a flood over in the Ohio Valley. A man and his boy were up on top of the chicken house. Water had come a way up. They saw up there a hat floating up and down. It would go up and come down and go up and come down. The father said, "I wonder what's the matter. What's that hat out there?" The boy said, "Well that's grandfather." "What do you mean, 'it's grandfather'?" "Well, I heard him say this morning before the floods come, he's gonna mow that yard, come hell or high water, and I guess he's out there."

Mental attitude. I don't think there's anything in the world that equals the importance of mental attitude. In this new book that I've just written for the purpose of conditioning the mind of patients for dentistry, you know in dentistry, gentlemen, about everything in the way of new techniques that could be thought of has been worked out, and the techniques in dentistry have just been well-nigh perfected. If there's anything that could be added there, I think you'd be hard put to the task of finding it. But the one thing that has not been done for you gentlemen in that profession is a system that conditions the mind of the patient not to be afraid. Now if I have really hit upon the right answer, then I will have done for your profession far more perhaps than I have ever done for any other profession on the face of the earth. Nothing would please me more because if there is one profession that I feel closest to, it's dentistry. I've been around dentistry all of my life, just missed being a dentist myself by a slight margin. My stepmother wanted me to become one too. I said, "Well, two in the family is one too many."

I want to tell you what a positive mental attitude is. This comes, now pardon me from reading; I don't often read, but this time I'm going to do it because it will save time, and the language that I have used here is just as succinct as anything I might give you orally. A positive mental attitude has many facets, and there are uncountable combinations for its application in connection with every circumstance that affects our lives. First of all, a positive mental attitude is the fixed purpose to make every experience, whether it is pleasant or unpleasant, yield some form of benefit that will help us to balance our lives with all the things that lead to peace of mind. In other words, if you've got a positive mental attitude everything that comes to you is beneficial whether it is good or bad, whether it's pleasant or unpleasant. You adjust yourself to it and do not go down under.

Now that's not hard to do, but that certainly is the first step that you have to take in adjusting yourself to the habit of a positive mental attitude. A positive mental attitude is the habit of searching for the seed of an equivalent advantage, which comes from every failure, defeat, or adversity we experience and the germination of that seed into something beneficial. Only a positive mental attitude can recognize and benefit by the seed of an equivalent benefit that comes with all unpleasant things that one experiences. A positive mental attitude is the only one that will recognize that a negative mental attitude will focus on the negative side of a circumstance that's unpleasant every time, and instead of doing something about it, will brood over it or become frustrated over it and become afraid of it. A positive mental attitude is the habit of keeping the mind busily engaged in connection with the circumstances and good desires in life and off the things one does not want.

Did you know, gentlemen, that the majority of people go all the way through life with their minds predominantly fixed upon the things they don't want: fear of poverty, fear of ill health, fear of the loss of loved ones, fear of criticism, fear of old age, fear of death; of all the things they don't want, and winding up in misery and poverty with the things that they've been thinking about most? Now isn't that correct? Doesn't that about state it? Look around you, if you please, and tell me whether or not the people that you can see are mostly successful or mostly unsuccessful; whether they are mostly happy or mostly unhappy. Have you ever in all of your life seen a perfectly happy man who has peace of mind because he knows what he wants? Have you ever seen such a man? The majority of people allow their minds to be occupied with too many things they don't want.

I personally resist the things I don't want; I put my mind on the things I do want, and I notice that those things I don't want, they starve to death. They just go away; go some other place. They go where they're wanted, where somebody will give them housing. I have no room in my mind for something I don't want and I'm not going to accept. There may be circumstances forced upon me that I've got to deal with, and that happens to everybody, but I can deal with them very much the way Mahatma Gandhi did. I can deal with them through passive resistance. I don't have to embrace them. I don't have to make them a part of myself if they're unpleasant. The mind has a definite way of clothing one's thoughts in appropriate physical equivalents. Think in terms of poverty and you will live in poverty. Think in terms of opulence and you will attract it through the eternal law of harmonious attraction. One's thoughts always clothe themselves in material things appropriate to their nature. A positive mental attitude is the habit of looking upon all unpleasant circumstances with which one meets as merely an opportunity for one to test his capacity to rise above.

My attitude toward my son's affliction was that I had been faced with one of the greatest tests of my philosophy that had ever come upon me, and I made up my mind that if I didn't meet that test successfully, I would burn up my manuscripts. I would never publish a book on the subject. I would never utter a word. If I couldn't make it work in my circumstances, I wouldn't tell other people that it could.

A positive mental attitude is the habit of evaluating all problems and distinguishing the difference between those that one can master and those that one cannot. If you've got a positive mental attitude, the first thing you do when a problem confronts you is to decide which category it belongs in. If it's something that you can do something about, start where you are, doing whatever you can. If it's something you can do nothing about, adjust yourself to it in passive resistance so that it does not throw you.

Now there are some circumstances that you can't control, but you can do something about all circumstances. You can refuse to embrace the ones you don't want. You can refuse to let them make you negative. You can refuse to let them scare you or fill you with fear. A positive mental attitude helps one to make allowances for the failures and the weaknesses of other people without becoming shocked by their negative-mindedness or being influenced by their way of thinking.

Now there are a lot of people who think that the world is going to hell just simply because the spotlight has been turned on Dick Nixon, and what I happen to know and I guess what every man in this room knows is, Dick Nixon, no matter what the outcome of it is, he's only doing what the vast majority of politicians have been doing on a much huger scale than anything that's been charged against him. I didn't see any applause on that one. I guess I don't know where I am. I didn't come up here to expound on religion or politics, and in mentioning Father Divine and Dick Nixon, I just use them as two outstanding examples because we all happen to be familiar with them.

Both have the habit of acting with definiteness of purpose with full belief in both the soundness of that purpose and one's ability to achieve it. That's what the person with a positive mental attitude does. He acts on definiteness of purpose with full belief in both the soundness of that purpose and his own ability to achieve.

When I was commissioned by Carnegie to give the world this philosophy, do you know the first thing I did carrying out a positive mental attitude? It will surprise you when I tell you. It was very little, but it was the only thing that I could do at that time, and I did it. I walked across the street from where I was talking to him to the public library, and I went in and I got a book and looked up the meaning of the word *philosophy*. I wasn't quite sure what it meant. Now that's how much prepared I was. Theoretically I have no right, no right to be standing here talking to you gentlemen today. No right to take up your time. Theoretically I have no right to have entered the minds of over sixty-five million people throughout two-thirds of the world. Theoretically I have no right to do that. Theoretically I have no right to have peace of mind, to have gained the freedoms, quit the things that keep men from having freedom. I have no right to this, but I did do it. I started in poverty, bound by poverty, bound by illiteracy, bound by fear, bound by worry, bound by superstition, and that's all I knew. It was all around me, and that's why I say that, theoretically, I have no right to be here. But I am here.

I have projected my influences into the lives of millions of people because I have maintained a positive mental attitude when the going was hard. Twenty years of it, the going was hard. Nobody recognized me. Everybody that heard what I was doing said I was a little bit cracked, a little bit off. There were times when I thought maybe they were right, but I kept on keeping on just the same, because there was something inherent, maybe, something inside of my soul that seemed to say that if you want a thing badly enough and don't change your mind about it, you're sure to get it, and that's not a bad principle of philosophy for anybody to embrace.

A positive mental attitude is the habit of going beyond the area of one's responsibility and rendering more service and better service than one is obligated to render and doing it in a friendly, pleasing mental attitude. I have never known any success, gentlemen, to be attained by anyone who didn't make it his business to go beyond the letter of his responsibility, to render more service and better service than he agreed to render, and do it in a pleasing mental attitude. And that applies in your profession just the same as it does in any other profession on the face of this earth. You can send patients away from your office so that every one of them becomes a walking advertisement for you, and while you're not permitted to advertise, don't you think that your patients will not advertise you?

Do you happen to know how much money was spent in getting *Think and Grow Rich* in circulation all over the world? Not one single red penny. That book has been distributed entirely by word of mouth, by people who read it, who liked it, and who told somebody else about it. Going the extra mile. A positive mental attitude is the habit of looking for the good qualities in other people and expecting to find them, but being prepared to recognize qualities that are not so good and not being shocked into a negative state of mind.

Now there are some people who are so deficient on this business of maintaining a positive mental attitude under all those circumstances, when they find a man who's made a mistake, a man who may have some little weakness, they just discount the whole man like that. You've got to learn to take people as you find them and to do the best you can in your relationship with them, dealing with their better qualities and shielding yourself as best you can against what you recognize to be the weak qualities. That's the way you've got to get along with people in this world. We're living in an age of chaos, an age of frustration, an age of disappointment and fear, and not without good reason for all this, and if we're going to get through it all, we've got to have a philosophy to live by, gentlemen. We've got to have a means of adjusting ourselves to the things that come up to destroy the patience and the faith of mankind. We've got to have a means of relating ourselves to it. And the means to that is the maintenance of a positive mental attitude.

Thank you, gentlemen, for inviting me to speak at your convention. It has been a pleasure and an honor. I hope I did not take too much of your time and that you learned something about the importance of your mental attitude.

(Applause)